Tax Answers at a Glance

08/09 TAX YEAR

Pat Joseph
Ashley Smith ACCA
Tim Smith FCA CTA
Iain Watson
Hugh Williams FCA

Tax Answers at a Glance
by Pat Joseph, Ashley Smith, Tim Smith, Iain Watson & Hugh Williams

1st edition 2001
2nd edition 2002
3rd edition 2003
4th edition 2004
5th edition 2005
6th edition 2006
7th edition 2007
8th edition 2008

© 2008 Lawpack Publishing

Lawpack Publishing Limited
76–89 Alscot Road
London SE1 3AW

www.lawpack.co.uk

ISBN: 978-1-905261-81-9

Crown Copyright forms are reproduced with the approval of HMSO.

Exclusion of Liability and Disclaimer

Contents

For Laurie Leask
1935 – 2007

'In this world nothing can be said to be certain, except death and taxes.'
Benjamin Franklin

Important facts

Welcome to *Tax Answers at a Glance*. It's packed with information and advice on your obligations and rights as a taxpayer.

The information this book contains has been carefully compiled from professional sources, but its accuracy is not guaranteed, as laws and regulations may change in the Budget and be subject to changing interpretations.

Tax regulations are stated as at 14 May 2008, after the emergency Budget.

Neither this nor any other publication can take the place of an accountant on important tax matters. Common sense should determine whether you need the assistance of an accountant rather than relying solely on the information in *Tax Answers at a Glance*.

About the authors

Pat Joseph is an Assistant Tax Manager at HM Williams Chartered Accountants; she has extensive experience in tax matters.

Ashley Smith ACCA is Assistant Tax Manager at HM Williams Chartered Accountants and is a Chartered Certified Accountant.

Tim Smith FCA CTA is Audit and Tax Partner at HM Williams.

Iain Watson is Tax Manager at HM Williams; formerly with HM Revenue & Customs, he offers an invaluable insider's view of tax legislation.

Hugh Williams FCA is Senior Partner at HM Williams, which he founded in 1973; he has written a number of professional books on tax and law.

Representing HM Williams, the authors were winners of the prestigious Butterworth Tolley Best Tax Team Award 2002. The firm was also awarded the coveted *Daily Telegraph*/Energis Customer Service Award 2001 in the Professional and Business Services, Small Organisation category.

Introduction

There are many books on tax, for both the professional and lay reader, but my impression is that most of them seem to look rather heavy, even if they are not. As a practising accountant I know only too well how clients will phone in with questions (perhaps quite simple questions) and all they want is a simple answer. If our clients are asking such questions, then there must be a lot of taxpayers who don't use the services of a professional accountant and who have similar questions that they would like answered.

Accordingly, this book is written almost in the style of a catechism. It's meant to home in on the questions, giving answers at a glance, rather than giving all the background information which, to be realistic, most taxpayers don't want or need.

The title 'Tax Answers at a Glance' came when I was talking about the concept to the London cabbie who was driving me away from Lawpack after it had commissioned me to write this book. 'Yeah, I can see that that would be a very useful book – one that gives tax answers at a glance.' So to that unnamed London taxi driver, I raise my hat in gratitude for giving us the title for this book.

I also must thank my fellow authors Pat Joseph, Ashley Smith, Tim Smith and Iain Watson, as well as Brian King of Christchurch Consultancy, who has helped us with the chapter on Inheritance Tax.

Our aim is for this book to be published on an annual basis and so, with these regular updates, there are bound to be more questions that readers would like us to answer than we have included in this latest edition. We would welcome contributions from our readership because their feedback will enable the next edition to be a further improvement on what we hope is already a sensible way of providing 'Tax Answers at a Glance'. If you have any comments or questions, please call us on 01752 334 950.

Hugh Williams

CHAPTER 1
Tax in general

What are the different taxes that we have to pay?

Between us (private individuals and businesses, etc.), we pay the following taxes:

- Income Tax
- National Insurance Contributions
- Value Added Tax
- Capital Gains Tax
- Inheritance Tax
- Stamp Duty
- Stamp Duty Land Tax
- Corporation Tax
- Petroleum Revenue Tax
- Fuel Duties
- Tobacco Duties
- Spirit Duties

- Wine Duties
- Beer and Cider Duties
- Betting and Gaming Duties
- Air Passenger Duties
- Insurance Premium Tax
- Landfill Tax
- Climate Change Levy
- Customs Duties and Levies
- Vehicle Excise Duties
- Oil Royalties
- Business Rates
- Council Tax

It's quite a list, isn't it? A summary of the actual tax rates and allowances is provided at Appendix 1.

How much does the Government raise in tax and what does it spend it on?

The Government expects to have raised, approximately, the following in tax in 2008/09:

	2008/09 £bn	2007/08 £bn	Selected percentages	Estimated average sum paid by each of us to the Government £
Income Tax	160	144	28%	3,076
Corporation Tax	52	49	9%	
Petroleum Revenue Tax	2	2		
Capital Gains Tax	5	3		96

Inheritance Tax	4	4		76
Stamp Duty	15	10		288
Value Added Tax	84	76	14%	1,615
Fuel Duties	27	25	5%	519
Tobacco Duties	8	8	1%	153
Spirit Duties	2	2		40
Wine Duties	2	2		40
Beer and Cider Duties	4	4		75
Betting and Gaming Duties	1	1		20
Air Passenger Duty	1	1		20
Insurance Premium Tax	2	2		40
Landfill Tax	1	1		
National Insurance	105	90	17%	2,019
Customs Duties and Levies	2	2		
HM Revenue & Customs	**477**	**426**	**82%**	
Vehicle Excise Duties	6	5	1%	115
Oil Royalties	1	1		
Business Rates	24	21	4%	
Council Tax	25	22	4%	480
Other taxes	11	10		
Total Other Receipts	**67**	**59**	**13%**	
Interest and adjustments	31	31	5%	
Total Receipts	**575**	**516**	**100%**	**£11,057** per head in 2008/09
On average each of us, adults and children, pays the Government	**£30.29**	**£27.19**		per day

We will pay over four per cent more in tax in 2008/09 than we did in 2007/08.

On the previous page we have seen that in 2008/09 the Government intends to raise £575 billion. The Government intends to spend £619 billion roughly as follows:

	£bn approx.
Health	111
Social Security	169
Public order and safety	33
Defence	33
Education	82
Interest	31
Housing	23
Transport	21
Social Services	27
Industry, agriculture, employment and training	22
Europe	15
Others	52
Total	619

When are the tax rates changed?

Recent governments have changed the method of deciding when tax rates should be changed (in other words, they have hopped about a bit), but, in principle, the announcements of the tax rates are given either in the pre-Budget report in the autumn or in the Budget statement in March. Those rates and allowances, etc. usually come into force on 6 April immediately following (but in 2007 the Chancellor announced a reduction in the basic rate of Income Tax and the abolition of the lower rate to take effect on 6 April 2008).

When it comes to National Insurance, these changes are also announced as part of the Chancellor's pre-Budget report in the autumn. This gives HM Revenue & Customs (HMRC) the chance to be prepared for the changes some months later.

The Chancellor has announced changes to other taxes for future years (i.e.

beyond the immediately succeeding year) in his main Budget in March and so, to a certain extent, tax advisers have known a few tax rates for a considerable period in advance.

What is the Income Tax year?

The Income Tax year runs from 6 April in one year to 5 April in the next. One of the authors of this book has spent a considerable amount of time badgering HMRC, Chancellors and Treasury officials to change this cumbersome system by using a more sensible date. Corporation Tax ends its financial years on 31 March and it would make sense for the Government to move the Income Tax year by a few days so that both tax year ends are coterminous. The reason the tax year ends on 5 April is not a logical one and so, at the back of this book we include a short postscript on why we should move to a more sensible date.

In the old days, and we are talking hundreds of years ago, the Income Tax year began on 25 March (the Feast of the Annunciation or Lady Day). Up to 1752 there were two European calendars operating using different days. Britain used the Julian Calendar, devised at the time of Julius Caesar, while the rest of the Continent (pretty well all the rest) used the Gregorian Calendar (introduced by Pope Gregory the Great), which meant that by the time we had reached 1752, the Continent was 11 days ahead of us. In that year the two calendars merged and Britain 'lost' 11 days. The Treasury said that it could not afford to lose 11 days and added 11 days on to the Income Tax year end. This meant that the Income Tax year in 1753 ended on 4 April.

In 1800, our Treasury, for some reason, thought that there was a leap year. The formula for leap years is that they are years which can be divided by four and, when there is a centenary year, when they can be divided by 400. 1800 could not be divided by 400 to give a whole number result and so it was not a leap year – our Treasury thought otherwise. So the Treasury added an extra day to the Income Tax year at that stage resulting in a tax year end of 5 April.

We said at the start that this answer wouldn't be a good one. We hope you agree with us that it's high time that this anachronism was changed. In fact, we can now let you know that it will be changed. HMRC decided in 2001 to do away with 5 April but it's not going to change until we adopt the Euro. At that stage we expect the new tax year to follow the calendar year. We are pleased with the announcement but not impressed with the lack of action.

What are business rates and Council Tax, and how is that money spent?

Business rates are the rates paid by businesses to central government via their local councils. They are like a tax, but they don't go towards local services, except as part of the Government's handout to local authorities. They are assessed on the area of space occupied by businesses.

Council Tax is collected by local councils and goes towards the following local services:

- Planning and economic development
- Recreation and tourism
- Environmental health
- Refuse collection
- Education
- Social services
- Police
- Fire

Council Tax is assessed on the market value of domestic properties, which are graded in bands from A to H. There is a 25 per cent discount where only one person lives in a property.

What is HM Revenue & Customs and what is the Treasury?

HM Revenue & Customs (HMRC) is the government department that is responsible for collecting most of the nation's taxes. HMRC advises the

Treasury on tax matters generally, but it's the Treasury, controlled by the Government in power at the time, that decides how much tax it wants to raise from taxpayers. It then works with HMRC to devise a system that enables that money to be collected.

Within HMRC, there are Inspectors of Taxes who check that the correct amount of tax is being paid by individuals, trusts and companies. There are also Collectors of Taxes, who make sure that the tax is paid.

Tax and civil partners

From 6 December 2005, same-sex couples have been able to register their relationship as civil partners. From this date, all the tax legislation that applies to married couples also applies to them. For instance, they are able to transfer assets to each other without incurring any Capital Gains Tax. However, if they have two main residences, they can only have one principal private residence exemption, so they may wish to consider making an election to nominate the main residence. They are also able to transfer assets to each other free of Inheritance Tax.

Throughout this book any reference to married couples includes civil partners.

What tax do I pay when I buy a motor car?

This is now a simple question to answer. New cars attract VAT at the standard rate (17.5 per cent). There is no special car tax, simply VAT.

You can only claim VAT back on the purchase of a car if:

- you are registered for VAT; and

- the vehicle is to be used exclusively for business purposes. This condition is virtually impossible to prove. The only people who can normally satisfy this condition are taxi drivers and driving instructors, and motor dealers who are buying the car as a stock item; or

- the vehicle is built to carry 12 or more seated persons and is to be used for business purposes.

The price of fuel has been going up alarmingly. As we went to press, this is how it's made up.

	Pence	Government	Fuel Companies	Credit Card Company	Garage Proprietor
Government	0.53	0.53			
Fuel production and distribution	0.35		0.35		
Garage proprietor	0.02				0.02
Credit card	0.03			0.03	
	0.93				
Add VAT	0.17	0.17			
Total per litre	**1.10**	**0.70**	**0.35**	**0.03**	**0.02**
	100%	**63%**	**32%**	**3%**	**2%**

So when you fill up with £65 of petrol:

£40.95 goes to the Government

£20.05 goes to the fuel companies

£1.95 goes to the credit card companies

£2.05 goes to the forecourt proprietor

So if you want to save tax, stop driving your car!

What tax do I pay when I buy fuel?

Let's say you have just paid £65 at the pump for fuel and used your credit card. How much of that amount goes to the Government, how much to the garage, how much to the fuel company and how much to the credit card people?

The answer is pretty staggering. More than £40 goes to the Government. Percentages vary depending on where you buy your fuel, but if you are paying 1.10p per litre, for example, the table opposite shows where your money goes.

What tax do I pay on celebratory fizz?

While the French pay only 4p duty per bottle of sparkling wine, in the UK we pay an enormous £1.87 per bottle. Analysis of a £3.99 bottle of Spanish Cava shows that Excise Duty and VAT account for £2.46 of the total retail cost.

First introduced by Lord Goschen in the reign of Queen Victoria as a luxury levy to raise funds for the navy, many would argue that this tax is now outdated and should be brought in line with the duty on still wine, which stands at £1.41 per bottle (compared with 2p per bottle in France).

The Wine and Spirit Trade Association (WSTA) is campaigning for the abolition of this tax differential, arguing that there is no reason why sparkling wine should be taxed differently to still wine.

Average price (pence)	Excise Duty (pence)	% duty in price	VAT rate	VAT (pence)	VAT + Duty (pence)
399	187	46.9%	17.50%	59.43	246.43

Source: The Wine and Spirit Trade Association (WSTA)

CHAPTER 2

Income Tax

What is Income Tax and what do we pay it on?

It may sound strange, but Income Tax is actually a temporary annual tax that the Government decides to keep going by means of an annual Finance Bill. It was introduced in 1799 as a means of financing the Napoleonic Wars, but even though those wars are well past, Income Tax still seems to be with us.

Income Tax used to be divided into schedules, but it now comes under headings and these are:

- Trade profits (including all business profits)
- Property income
- Savings and investment income
- Miscellaneous income (covers income not falling under the other headings)
- Earnings and pension income (which includes taxable social security benefits)

It might be more relevant if we now look at what income is not taxed (i.e. what is tax free):

- Adoption Allowances
- Adult Placement Carers' Income
- Annuities from gallantry awards
- Attendance Allowance
- Bereavement Payments
- Betting, lottery and pools winnings, and raffle prizes
- Car parking benefits
- Child Benefit
- Child dependency additions
- Child Tax Credit
- Child Trust Funds
- Christmas bonuses paid by the state to pensioners
- Compensation for loss of employment of up to £30,000 (professional advice must be sought)
- Compensation for mis-sold personal pensions
- Council Tax Benefit
- Damages and compensation for personal injury, including interest
- Disability Living Allowance
- Educational Maintenance Allowance
- Foster Care Income
- Gifts for employees from third parties if they are under £250 a year
- Gratuities and bounties from the armed forces
- Guardian's Allowance
- Home improvement, repair and insulation grants
- Housing Benefit
- Incapacity Benefit (short-term – lower rate)
- Incentives for electronic communications
- Income Support
- Individual Savings Accounts (ISAs)
- Industrial injury benefits
- Insurance bond withdrawals of up to five per cent per year (this can be complicated and professional advice should be sought)
- Insurance policy payments (mortgage payment protection, permanent health, etc.)
- Interest from National Savings Certificates
- Interest on overpaid tax
- Interest on Tax Reserve Certificates
- Invalidity pensions

- Jobfinder's Grant
- Jobseeker's Allowance
- Life assurance policy bonuses and profits
- Long-service awards of up to £50 for each year of service (for employees)
- Lump sums from an approved pension scheme
- Luncheon vouchers of up to 15p per day but cash would be taxable – this sum hasn't changed for 40 years!
- Maintenance or alimony payments
- Maternity Allowance
- Miners' Coal Allowance
- National Savings Bank interest of up to £70 per person on ordinary accounts. These accounts are no longer available but the exemption applies to existing account holders
- National Savings Certificates' increase in value
- Pension Credit
- Pensions from Austria or Germany to victims of Nazi persecution
- Personal equity plans (PEPs)
- Premium bond prizes
- Provident benefits paid by a trade union of up to £4,000 for lump-sum payments
- Purchased life annuities – capital element only
- Rent-a-room relief up to £4,250 a year
- Save As You Earn Schemes (SAYE) bonuses and interest
- Scholarship income and bursaries
- Severe Disablement Allowances
- Share option profits made under an SAYE option scheme – Capital Gains Tax may be payable
- Shares awarded under an approved Share Incentive Plan (professional advice must be sought)
- Social fund payments
- Statutory Redundancy Pay
- Strike and unemployment pay from a trade union
- Student Grants
- Suggestion scheme awards
- Training allowances for reserve forces
- Travel to work on a works bus
- TV licence payment

- Vaccine damage payment
- Venture Capital Trust dividends
- War Disablement Benefits
- War Widows' Pension
- Winter fuel payments
- Woodlands
- Working Tax Credit

What is an annual Income Tax Return?

This is a form issued each year to about nine million taxpayers, the purpose of which is for them to list their income and, if they wish to do it themselves, calculate the overall tax due and the dates by which it should be paid. It can now be completed and submitted online.

Some taxpayers (mostly employees and pensioners) are now being issued with a shorter, simpler Tax Return. The taxpayer won't need to calculate their own liability, even if the Tax Return is submitted to HM Revenue & Customs (HMRC) after 30 September.

Paper Tax Returns must be filed by 31 October or you will face a £100 penalty. Returns filed online must reach the Tax Office by 31 January.

How do I know if I have to fill out a Tax Return and how do I get hold of one?

You will have to complete a Tax Return if you:

- are self-employed;

- are in partnership;

- are in receipt of income from land and property;

- are a director;

- incur taxable capital gains;

- are sent one (if HMRC issues a Tax Return, it has to be completed by the taxpayer).

If you are in any doubt, you should go to your local Tax Office, advise it of your circumstances, and get it to confirm whether you should fill out a Tax Return.

If you need to get hold of a Tax Return, then you should contact the local Tax Office and ask it to send you one (better still, visit the offices).

A checklist of what to keep for your Tax Return is provided at Appendix 2.

What are Child Tax Credits and Working Tax Credits?

Warning: the whole subject of tax credits is extremely complicated. We have done our best to reduce it to its simplest elements but reading the following section needs a clear head.

Working Tax Credit (WTC) is for those with low incomes. It's a means-tested payment to top up the earnings of those in work. The qualifying conditions are as follows:

- You must work at least 16 hours a week if you have children or a disability, or are aged 50 plus and returning to work after a period on certain benefits.

- If you don't have children or a disability, you must be over 25 and working at least 30 hours a week.

Your total entitlement is calculated by adding together the basic element and any additional elements to which you are entitled.

WTC is paid directly to the person who is working 16 or more hours a week. Couples where both work 16 hours or more a week may choose which of them will receive it.

Child Tax Credits are paid directly to the main carer of the child or children. It's designed to combine the child support elements of the old Working Family Tax Credits, Income Support, Jobseeker's Allowance and Children's Tax Credit.

CTC can be claimed by families with at least one child, with an annual family income of up to £58,000. It provides support for:

- children until 1 September after their 16th birthday;

- children aged 16 to 19 who are in full-time 'non-advanced' education (i.e. studying for at least 12 hours a week and the course leads to A level, NVQ level 3, or below) and also those receiving approved training under unwaged work-based training programmes;

- children aged 16 to 19 who have left full-time education but don't have a job or training place and have registered with the Careers Service or Connexions Service, and are not claiming Income Support or tax credits in their own right.

What if my circumstances change?

You **must** tell the Tax Credit Office if:

- you marry or live with someone as a couple;

- you separate;

- you stop paying for childcare for at least four weeks, or childcare costs reduce by £10 a week for at least four weeks in a row.

You should tell it about the birth of a new child or when a child leaves full-time education. You should also tell it if your hours change to less than 16 a week or more than 29 hours a week. It's advisable to notify the Tax Office if your income increases by £25,000. A decrease in income should also be reported. These changes are important as any increase in tax credits will only be backdated for up to three months whereas any decrease will be backdated to the date of the change.

What next?

HMRC will be renewing awards for the year ending 5 April 2009 and finalising new awards for the year ending 5 April 2008.

Credits for the year ending 5 April 2009 will be based on income for the year ending 5 April 2008. The following should be noted:

- If requested, details of income and circumstances should be submitted by 31 July 2008.

- The details you provide should relate to the period of the claim, which may not necessarily coincide with the tax year; for instance, if you had a baby during the year.

If you only receive the family element of CTC, you won't be asked to provide details of income and your claim will carry on as before. However, if your circumstances have changed, you must notify the Tax Credit Office. Remember, any increases in credits are only backdated for three months.

You can request a claim form by telephoning 0845 300 3900 or you can apply online at www.hmrc.gov.uk.

How do I work out how much tax I have to pay and when to pay it?

If you have to complete a Tax Return, included in the package will be a tax calculation guide for you to follow. It's not within the scope of this book to guide you through it (HMRC's form does it pretty well for you), but the main thing to bear in mind is that if you get your Tax Return submitted by 30 September each year, HMRC will work out for you how much tax you have to pay and when you have to pay it.

In principle, you make two payments a year. On 31 January each year you will pay the balance of the previous year's tax still owing plus one half of the previous year's tax liability as a first payment on account for the following year.

On 31 July each year you will pay the second half of last year's tax liability as a second payment on account. On 31 January following, you will find yourself paying any balance of tax that is due plus another payment on account based on this year's total tax bill and so on.

If this all sounds very confusing, don't worry, it is! The Government introduced self-assessment in 1997 with the intention that tax recording and calculations should be so simple that anybody could do it. If you ask most professional accountants nowadays, they would say that the current tax rules are so complicated they would find it very difficult to work out your tax liability if they didn't have the services of a computer.

What self-assessment has done is remove a lot of the work that was previously done in Tax Offices and dump it either on the taxpayer's own desk or, if the taxpayer is prepared to pay for it, in the offices of professional accountants, who now do the work that the Inspectors of Taxes formerly did.

In other words, self-assessment doesn't mean a simple calculation. It means 'It's up to you, mate, and don't blame us if we, HMRC, have made it difficult!'

What if my tax payments are late?

An interest charge is:

- automatic on late paid Income Tax, Class 4 National Insurance contributions and Capital Gains Tax;
- added to existing liabilities and treated as tax due and payable.

A surcharge applies to all amounts due in respect of the previous tax year on 31 January following the end of that tax year and not paid by 28 February. This is five per cent of the amount unpaid more than 28 days after the due date with a further five per cent of the amount unpaid more than six months after the due date. However, the taxpayer may appeal against a surcharge if they have a reasonable excuse.

What happens if I fail to complete a Tax Return on time?

If you are preparing a Tax Return, there is an automatic fixed £100 penalty (or 100 per cent of the unpaid tax if less) if your Tax Return is not filed by the statutory filing date, 31 January in the following year. There is a further fixed £100 penalty if the Return is not filed six months after the statutory filing date, i.e. following 31 July.

In addition, there are daily penalties (maximum £60 per day) which can be levied, but HMRC has to obtain a ruling from the Tax Commissioners first.

Tax-geared penalties may also be imposed where the tax is paid more than one month late.

What can I set against my tax bill?

There is no quick answer to this question because there is a whole range of deductions, allowances, reliefs and expenses that taxpayers can claim. In principle, everybody is entitled to a personal allowance (and there are a number of different types of personal allowance, including increased allowances for the elderly), but apart from that it all depends on your circumstances. The sorts of relief that we, as accountants, see our clients claiming and that we can claim on their behalf are as follows:

- Relief for losses in a business
- Relief for personal pension contributions
- Relief for Gift Aid payments
- Relief for investments made under either the Venture Capital Trust or Enterprise Investment Schemes
- Blind Person's Allowance
- Relief for interest borrowed for certain purposes
- Business expenses
- Certain allowances against capital gains

We do advise you to read HMRC's guidance notes that come with your Tax Return carefully to be sure that you are claiming all of your relief, but it simply isn't possible to list them all in the space of a book that gives you quick and easy to comprehend answers.

What is the difference between earned and unearned income?

About 30 years ago it was better to be in receipt of earned income than unearned income because unearned income attracted investment income surcharge and there was a special earned income relief.

Nowadays it's better to be in receipt of unearned income because earned income (salaries, wages, benefits, etc.) is not only taxable but is also subject to National Insurance contributions.

The distinction between the two is not a key one nowadays, but one of the more obvious distinctions arises in the case of a director shareholder. If they are paid a salary, then both the company and the director must pay National Insurance contributions on that salary. The payment of £1,000 as earnings may result in about 40 per cent of that figure going to the Government. If that same person is paid a dividend out of taxed profits, no further tax will be due to the Government although, in due course, there will be tax payable by the director when it comes to completing the personal Tax Return, if they are a higher rate taxpayer.

Personal reliefs and allowances

The rates of the various personal reliefs and allowances for 2008/09 are as follows:

	£
Personal	6,035
Blind person's	1.800

Age	
Personal (age 65–74)	9,030
Married couple's (age 65–74) and born before 6 April 1935	*6,535
Personal (age 75 and over)	9,180
Married couple's (age 75 and over) and born before 6 April 1935	*6,625

* indicates allowances where tax relief is restricted to ten per cent

What tax relief can I claim against my payments of interest?

Opportunities to claim tax relief on payments of interest on loans are limited and are now restricted to the following:

- buying a share in a partnership or contributing capital to a partnership if you are a partner;

- buying shares in a close company (see page 118) or lending capital to it;

- buying plant and machinery for use in a job or partnership.

The interest paid (and not the capital) is deducted from your total income in the year of payment.

Can I get tax relief on my mortgage?

Unfortunately, since 5 April 2000, tax relief on mortgage interest payments has been withdrawn; this applies to both interest paid under MIRAS (mortgage interest relief at source) and otherwise. But see 'What is the tax wheeze for buy-to-let investors?' on page 90.

Is there a right time to get married for Income Tax purposes?

The Married Couple's Allowance was withdrawn on 6 April 2000, except for those couples where either the husband or wife was aged 65 or more at 5 April 2000.

However, if you get married and you were over 65 on 5 April 2000 or your spouse was, you can claim 1/12th of the allowance for each month of the tax year concerned, starting with the month of marriage. So there is no 'best time' to get married for Income Tax purposes.

Is there a right time to get divorced or separated for Income Tax purposes?

For those who are still able to claim the Married Couple's Allowance, this is not reduced in the year when couples separate or in the year of death of either spouse. However, with it being so restricted as to its use, this matter is now of little consequence to parties when they divorce or separate.

What happens to someone's Income Tax affairs when they die?

When someone dies, they are entitled to their normal full year's worth of allowances. A Tax Return will need to be completed for the last period of life from 6 April up to the date of death and the tax worked out accordingly.

Income arising after death is treated as the income of the estate and becomes the responsibility of the trustees or executors. When the estate is distributed, both the capital and the income that has arisen since the date of death will be distributed according to the Will to the various beneficiaries and tax will be deducted from any income that has been received at the appropriate rate.

If you, as a beneficiary, are in receipt of income that has been credited to a deceased person's estate, then you will receive that income net of the appropriate rate tax and while you may have to pay higher rate tax on the income, there is also a chance that you might be able to claim some back or for there to be no adjustment at all.

What should one do about the income of children and Income Tax?

Children, from the moment they are born, are entitled to a personal allowance and if they are in receipt of net income, apart from dividends, they are almost certainly entitled to a repayment of tax. Accordingly, where children are in receipt of income from which tax has been deducted, it's potentially refundable. Get a tax claim form from the Tax Office (note that it's called a 'tax claim' and not a Tax Return, but it amounts to the same thing). When you have completed it and sent it in, HMRC will either send a cheque in favour of the child or make a refund of tax straight to that child's own bank or building society account. The parent can also receive the refund on the child's behalf.

What are the most sensible sorts of investment for children for tax purposes?

The simplest answer is that savings accounts with building societies or banks that are in the children's names should pay the children interest gross (i.e. without tax deducted).

It's still quite permissible for children to hold shares in companies, even though the tax credits on the dividends are not refundable.

If the children don't have any investments and if the parents have surplus after-tax income of their own which they give to their children, this is usually tax free in the children's hands and, if the parents are particularly wealthy, is a very useful way of transferring income to them, so that the children can accumulate a sum that can then be invested. However, once the income from the source exceeds £100 p.a. it will be taxed in the hands of the parents. Where parents transfer their own shares to their children, if the children are under 18, the income arising on these shares will be regarded as belonging to the parents, so this doesn't save tax.

The Child Trust Fund is a tax-free savings scheme designed for children. The Government contributes £250 when the child is born and a further £250 (£500 for lower-income families) at the age of seven. Parents, family and friends can contribute a further £1,200 annually. The child is entitled to the fund at the age of 18 and there will be no restriction on how they use the money.

What are the rules for charitable giving and Income Tax?

- Gifts of money to charities attract tax relief under the Gift Aid scheme. The gift is treated as if it had been made after deduction of Income Tax at the basic rate. So if you give £80 to a charity, it can get £20 tax back. If you are a higher rate taxpayer, you can claim a further £20 of tax relief in your Tax Return.

- The Gift Aid certificate has been replaced by a simpler and more flexible Gift Aid declaration. If you turn to Appendix 5 you will see an example of this and how it works. However, remember this will only work if you have paid more tax than will be reclaimed by the charity. Otherwise, HMRC will send you a bill for the difference.

- There is a generous tax relief for gifts of certain investments and property to charity.

What is 'Payroll Giving'?

If their employer is registered under the Payroll Giving Scheme, employees can arrange a regular deduction from their pre-tax pay to go to a nominated charity, church or charitable association.

Employers need to sign an administration contract with an authorised Payroll Giving Agency. They do make a small administration charge that is either deducted from the donation or can be paid separately by the employer (around four to five per cent).

How do I reclaim overpaid tax?

If you are likely always to pay too much tax (through receiving no gross income, i.e. all your income suffers tax at source), HMRC will spot this and will no longer send you a form called a Tax Return, but a tax claim form instead. It amounts to the same thing but will probably be returnable to a Tax Office that deals solely with tax repayments.

If, on the other hand, you normally pay tax but in a certain year discover that you have overpaid, you can allocate some or all of your repayment to a charity – again, tick the relevant box on the Return. If you tick the appropriate box on that Tax Return, you can claim for the money to be refunded to you. If you leave the overpayment unrefunded, it will go to reduce your future year's tax payments.

What are the rules regarding pre-owned assets?

A free-standing tax charge applies to the benefit people get from the free or low-cost enjoyment of assets they formerly owned or provided the funds to purchase.

The charge applies to both tangible (land, property, possessions, etc.) and intangible assets.

This will primarily affect people who have entered into 'contrived arrangements' to dispose of valuable assets while retaining the ability to use them. This is most frequently encountered in Inheritance Tax avoidance schemes where property is given away.

There are specific exceptions to the charge:

- The property ceased to be owned before 18 March 1986.

- The property formerly owned is currently owned by your spouse.

- The property was sold at open market value and paid for in cash.

- The asset still forms part of the individual's estate for Inheritance Tax purposes under the Gift with Reservation rules.

- The asset was only owned by virtue of an inheritance which has subsequently been varied by agreement with the beneficiaries (i.e. a deed of variation).

- Any enjoyment of the asset is incidental, or arises after an out-and-out gift to a family member and comes to the benefit of the donor because of unforeseen changes in the donor's circumstances.

The amount of the tax charge will be based on the rental value for land and property, and five per cent of capital value for possessions and intangible assets, subject to a de minimis limit of £5,000.

As it may be impossible to withdraw from potentially complex transactions from the past, an election can be made to have the value of the asset included in the estate for Inheritance Tax purposes. This will avoid a tax charge becoming due.

What might be the effect on my Council Tax banding if I work from home and use my home as an office?

If you are an employee, so long as your employer agrees that you can work from home (and whether or not your employer provides you with equipment to carry out such work), you may be entitled to seek a reduction in Council Tax on the ground that the room you use as an office can no longer be used, for example as a bedroom. It would be advisable for you not to hold business meetings at your home, because too many of those might constitute a change of use and cause other problems with your local council.

You may be interested to learn that one local council, having reduced the amount of Council Tax payable on such a house, sought to impose business rates on the part of the house used for business purposes. However, it failed in its endeavours and the local valuation office decided not to proceed with the case.

CHAPTER 3

National Insurance

What is National Insurance?

National Insurance contributions are an extra and important tax that has to be paid on certain sources of income. The contributions paid are, in principle, used to pay for an individual's following state benefits:

- State Retirement Pension
- Bereavement Allowance
- Bereavement Payment
- Widowed Parent's Allowance
- Maternity Allowance
- Incapacity Benefit
- Jobseeker's Allowance

What are the different classes of National Insurance?

There are four classes of National Insurance and some have sub-divisions.

- **Class 1** – is paid by employers and employees on employees' earnings. Class 1A is paid on employees' benefits in kind. (See also 'What National Insurance is payable on employees' benefits?', page 56.) Class 1B is paid where the employer decides to pay the tax on employees' benefits under a so-called PAYE Settlement Agreement.

- **Class 2** – is paid by the self-employed (but also see Class 4).

- **Class 3** – is a voluntary contribution which you can pay in order to protect your benefits, if you are not otherwise paying National Insurance contributions (e.g. this might arise because you have no earnings on which National Insurance is payable, but you still want to pay for a state pension).

- **Class 4** – is an additional National Insurance contribution paid by the self-employed whose earnings exceed a certain sum. Class 4 contributions don't provide any further benefits for the contributor.

You won't have to pay National Insurance contributions if you have retired or passed normal retirement age (60 for a woman, 65 for a man). However, if you are still working beyond the age of 65, your employer still remains liable for its National Insurance contributions.

Who pays what?

National Insurance – the basic facts for 2008/09

1. Employees pay 11 per cent of their earnings between £105 per week and £770 per week, and one per cent on all earnings over that figure.

2. Employers pay 12.8 per cent on their employees' earnings over £105 per week. There is no upper limit.

3. The self-employed pay £2.30 per week.

4. In addition, self-employed people with profits over £5,435 pay eight per cent on all profits between £5,435 and £40,040, and one per cent on all profits over that figure.

5. Self-employed people with low earnings (less than £4,825 in 2008/09) can elect not to pay National Insurance but this is not a good idea unless contributions are being paid on other sources of income.

6. Men over 65, women over 60 and children under 16 pay nothing. However, employers still have to pay up to 12.8 per cent on their earnings.

7. If you don't come into any of the above categories (i.e. if you are going abroad), you can elect to pay £8.10 a week in order to maintain your contributions record.

Note: items 1 and 2 are called Class 1; 3 and 5 are Class 2; 7 is Class 3 and 4 is Class 4.

What do I get for my money?

The table below gives you an indication of what the different classes of National Insurance contributions pay for:

Type of Benefit	Class 1 (Employed)	Class 2 (Self-employed)	Class 3 (Voluntary)
Retirement Pension Basic	Yes	Yes	Yes
Retirement Pension Additional	Yes	No	No
Bereavement Allowance	Yes	Yes	Yes
Bereavement Payment	Yes	Yes	Yes
Widowed Parent's Allowance	Yes	Yes	Yes
Maternity Allowance	Yes	Yes	No
Incapacity Benefit	Yes	Yes	No
Jobseeker's Allowance	Yes	No	No

How are National Insurance contributions paid?

- **Class 1** contributions are paid on a weekly or monthly basis by the employer (secondary contributions). The employer deducts their employees' contributions (primary contributions) from their gross pay (along with Income Tax and other deductions) and pays that sum over, together with their own contributions, by the 19th of the following month.

- **Class 2** contributions are paid by monthly direct debit or quarterly in arrears.

- **Class 3** contributions are paid by monthly direct debit.

- **Class 4** contributions are calculated along with the self-employed's Self-Assessment Income Tax calculation and paid once or twice a year, with the Income Tax payments. (This applies to any Class 4 contribution.)

How do I find my National Insurance number?

If you don't know your National Insurance number, write to your local Jobcentre (whose address and telephone number you will find in the telephone book) and ask it to give you your National Insurance number, telling it your:

- full name
- maiden name
- date of birth
- date of marriage
- present address

If you need to apply for a National Insurance number, you will be asked to attend an interview and prove your identity.

What happens if I should be paying National Insurance contributions but fail to do so?

Make no mistake, this can be expensive if you start up either as an employer who fails to deduct tax and National Insurance contributions from your employees' wages, or you start in self-employment and fail to register with HM Revenue & Customs (HMRC).

If, as an employer, you fail to pay over the correct National Insurance contributions for your employees by 19 April following the end of the tax year, not only will these have to be paid over, but in addition there will be interest due on the late payment and, in addition to that, there will be penalties for failing to make the payments on time.

If you are an employee whose employer is failing to deduct contributions from your pay and pay them over to HMRC, you cannot be held liable to make the payment yourself. It's the employer's responsibility. Our understanding of the law is that, since it's the employer's responsibility, there is no way in which HMRC can get you to pay the National Insurance contributions that should have been deducted from your gross pay nor should your benefits be affected, because HMRC will collect the contributions from your employer.

HMRC is responsible for National Insurance contributions. The application forms for the newly self-employed are designed in such a way that the National Insurance obligations are dealt with at the same time as registering for tax under self-assessment. Where earnings are below the small earnings exception threshold and you decide that you don't wish to pay contributions (but see 6 on page 29), you must apply for an exception certificate. This can be done at the same time as registration or at any time later.

Where existing self-employed people are not paying the appropriate contributions, they could be made to catch up and the outstanding payments could be subject to interest and penalties. HMRC can claw back contributions without a time limit. Contrast this with the situation where you have been claiming exemption, but realise that you would be better off if you were to pay contributions. As an individual you can only catch up with the last six years of contributions.

Once Class 4 contributions have been calculated on your Tax Return they become part of your overall tax liability and are thereafter no longer separately identified. Unpaid contributions are treated in the same way as unpaid tax.

What should I do if I'm worried that my National Insurance contributions are not up to date?

You should contact the National Insurance Contributions Office and find out exactly where you stand with regard to contributions you have made and benefits you are entitled to. This is called a Retirement Pension Forecast.

What is Class 4 National Insurance?

This is the extra National Insurance 'tax' that has to be paid by the self-employed when their earnings exceed a certain threshold. It's an additional tax, and tax is the right word because it actually buys no further benefits for the payer. It's calculated as part of the self-assessment tax and Class 4 National Insurance calculation and paid with Income Tax on the same dates as Income Tax.

What if I have paid too much National Insurance?

People with either multiple employments or employment and self-employment no longer have a specific maximum level of contributions. Instead, the legislation provides a formula and each individual will have their own individualised Class 1 and Class 2 maximum figures. Examples of how these maxima are calculated are available on HMRC's website (www.hmrc.gov.uk). Refunds can generally be claimed for the last six contribution years if applicable.

If I am self-employed and have not been paying National Insurance, what are the chances I will get away with it?

One consequence of the merger of HMRC and the Contributions Agency is that the power to charge interest and penalties on unpaid National Insurance Contributions will now be used.

Information is now much more likely to be shared. For example, HMRC is making its list of self-employed people available to National Insurance inspectors.

It has not gone unnoticed that there are far more self-employed taxpayers than there are Class 2 contributors, even after taking account of those with small earnings exception certificates.

If you are self-employed and are not paying Class 2 National Insurance contributions, you will be found out. The consequences are:

1. You may get a bill for the unpaid contributions.

2. A penalty may be imposed.

3. You could be subject to a criminal prosecution.

4. You are diminishing your entitlement to a state pension.

There is also the minefield of Class 1, 1A and 1B contributions for remuneration, expenses, benefits in kind and PAYE Settlement Agreements. Do you know which to pay and when payments are due? The rules are complex and the consequences of getting it wrong could be expensive. Have you ever been 'invited' to make voluntary (Class 3) National Insurance contributions and wondered whether you should? Maybe your contribution record is incomplete. In such circumstances, it's best to get your record corrected as it can make a big difference to your benefit/pension entitlement.

If you have a problem, or wish to avoid one, the sooner you start the better. Corrections can only be made for the last six contribution years!

CHAPTER 4

Employment and Income Tax

What do I do if I employ somebody?

Taking somebody on can be one of the early big milestones in any business. What follows can also apply to private individuals who are employing people such as cooks, nannies, gardeners, etc. and so, while most of what follows relates to the things that a business person should do, private individuals should be aware that they may well be caught by the PAYE regulations that relate to employing people.

There is no easy answer to this very simple question. Having said this, the only answer is that you have to obey the law but knowing what the law is is not always easy in itself.

If you take on somebody and you are paying them more than £105 a week, no matter what their age, you have to pay National Insurance contributions and the rate is 12.8 per cent. If this is the case, then the first thing you should do is inform HM Revenue & Customs (HMRC) that you have taken somebody on. You can do this by calling the New Employer Helpline on 0845 607 0143. The second thing you should do is decide how you are going to handle the PAYE payment obligations. In our view, the simplest way of meeting your obligations is to ask a professional accountant to look after the PAYE side of things for you. They will tell you how much to pay your employees net of tax and National Insurance and they will also send you the appropriate PAYE slip for making the monthly or quarterly payments to HMRC. They will also be able to help you with the Annual Return (P35) and with the benefit forms (P11Ds).

A second alternative is to buy a simple computer program and do the work in-house yourself. These are good, economically priced and well worth the investment in both software and stationery.

A third alternative is to use the manual forms HMRC send you. In our view, these are not easy forms to follow and are definitely a worse option than the first two suggestions above.

A fourth alternative is to go and buy a manual wages system from the local stationer. This would certainly be better than using HMRC's forms but, in this computer centred age, we certainly recommend options 1 and 2.

If you take on someone earning more than £90 per week and less than £105 per week, National Insurance contributions won't be due, but you should complete a P14 for them as they qualify for National Insurance credits.

If you take on someone earning less than £105 per week, there will be no National Insurance contributions to worry about. However, you may still find that you need to deduct tax from their earnings. This depends on the tax code you have been directed to use, which is either shown on the Form P45 from their previous job or advised by HMRC. If you take on someone who doesn't have a P45 (because they weren't working previously or they have an existing job which is to continue), they will need to complete P46 and send it to HMRC. It will then send you a notice of coding, which may well direct you to deduct tax if there are other earnings.

We said at the start that there is no easy answer to this and perhaps the best answer to give you is to go and discuss the matter with HMRC or with a professional accountant. Make no mistake, it's a complicated business and one that is very important to get right. Employers should not turn a blind eye to their obligations.

Is the person I'm taking on an employee or self-employed?

As with the above question there is no easy answer to this. There have been many painful cases brought to light by a visiting HMRC PAYE investigator. Employers who thought that all their people were self-employed have discovered to their horror and great expense that they should have been deducting tax and National Insurance from the gross payments that they have been making to their staff.

Below you will find a list of questions that you should ask which will help you decide whether the person whose services you are using is self-employed or an employee.

As practising accountants we are of the opinion that, if somebody is 'employed' on a regular basis, but is regarded by both parties as self-employed (and the following questionnaire justifies this decision), a contract should be signed by both parties which can be shown to HMRC and which clearly establishes that the arrangement is one of self-employment.

Employed or self-employed? A questionnaire to help you decide

HMRC is keen to classify self-employed people as employees because this increases National Insurance contributions and Income Tax.

How can you tell if someone is an employee or is self-employed? Answering the following questions should help. Note: there are separate and new rules for workers in the construction industry; the following questions are not appropriate for such workers.

1. Is there a contract of service, i.e. a contract of employment?

   A 'no' answer indicates self-employment.

2. Is there a contract for services, i.e. a notice supplied by the person carrying out the work (A), indicating the nature of goods or services they will provide to B (this need not be written)?

   A 'yes' answer indicates self-employment.

3. Is the person who does the work in business on their own account?

   A 'yes' answer indicates self-employment.

4. If the person is in business on their own account, has evidence been

provided that this is indeed the case (e.g. copy accounts, the payment of Class 2 National Insurance contributions)?

A 'yes' answer indicates self-employment.

5. Are the hours worked decided by the person doing the work?

A 'yes' answer indicates self-employment.

6. Are the days worked decided by the person doing the work?

A 'yes' answer indicates self-employment.

7. Does the person doing the work decide when to take their own holidays?

A 'yes' answer indicates self-employment.

8. Does the business proprietor supervise the work?

A 'no' answer indicates self-employment.

9. Is the person part and parcel of the business?

A 'no' answer indicates self-employment.

10. Does the person supply tools and/or materials when they carry out the work?

A 'yes' answer indicates self-employment.

11. Does the person doing the work give the business an invoice for the work done?

A 'yes' answer indicates self-employment.

12. Does the business calculate how much to pay the person doing the work and give a payslip?

A 'no' answer indicates self-employment.

13. Is self-employment the intention of both parties?

A 'yes' answer indicates self-employment.

14. Is the person bound by the customer care credo of the business?

A 'no' answer indicates self-employment.

15. Is the person carrying out the work required to wear a uniform or dress tidily at the diktat of the business?

A 'no' answer indicates self-employment.

16. Is the person carrying out the work provided with a car or transport by the business?

A 'no' answer indicates self-employment.

17. In the event of sickness, does the business continue to pay the person while not at work?

A 'no' answer indicates self-employment.

18. Is the person carrying out the work at liberty to work for other businesses?

A 'yes' answer indicates self-employment.

19. Is the person carrying out the work required to work in order to perform a specific task?

A 'yes' answer indicates self-employment.

20. Does the business, on asking this person to carry out work for it, assume any responsibility or liability characteristic of an employment, such as employment protection, employees' liability, pension entitlements, etc.?

A 'no' answer indicates self-employment.

21. Is the person who does the work paid an agreed price per job?

A 'yes' answer indicates self-employment (i.e. they are not paid for the hours they work, but for the work carried out).

22. Is the work carried out regularly?

A 'no' answer indicates self-employment.

23. Does the individual work for other people?

A 'yes' answer indicates self-employment.

24. Does the person carrying out the work advertise?

A 'yes' answer indicates self-employment.

25. Does the person carrying out the work have headed stationery?

A 'yes' answer indicates self-employment.

26. Can the person send a substitute? If so, has this ever happened?

A 'yes' answer indicates self-employment.

27. Does the person have to rectify faulty workmanship in their own time and at their own expense?

A 'yes' answer indicates self-employment.

Having addressed these questions, you should now begin to know whether in reality the person under consideration is an employee or is self-employed. However, a definite answer can only be given by the courts.

What if I take on someone part-time or casually?

This is probably the most difficult employment question of all to answer. The typical accountant's answer is 'it all depends'. Our view is that if you read the three preceding questions, you will get a pretty good idea of your obligations. If you take on someone casually on both an infrequent, irregular (possibly one-off) basis, HMRC is very unlikely to be concerned about the matter. There is a very well-known legal maxim, 'de minimis non curat lex', which means 'the law is not concerned with trifles'. The authors think that the best advice we can give to the reader is to say, 'Is this a trifle?' If it is, and you can justify it as being so to a visiting inspector, then regard the person as being casual – a trifle. If the matter has obviously some regularity and (shall we say) meaty content – in other words not a trifle – then we suggest that you go and talk it through with HMRC or an accountant and take the action that arises from such an approach.

What is PAYE?

PAYE stands for Pay As You Earn. It represents a logical system whereby week by week or month by month an employer deducts tax in such a way that, at the end of the income tax year, the right amount of tax has been deducted and handed over to the authorities. It works in the following way:

Let us say that you earn £15,000 a year and your personal allowance is £3,000. Let us also suppose that the rate of tax that you are paying is ten per cent (wouldn't that be nice?).

If you paid your tax just once a year you would calculate the tax as follows:

- £15,000 less your tax-free personal allowance £3,000 gives you...
- Taxable pay £12,000 on which...
- Tax @ ten per cent is £1,200.

The way PAYE works is to collect that £1,200 on a monthly basis and that works as follows:

HMRC issues tables that show the tax-free pay for each of the various PAYE codes for each week and for each month throughout the year. It also issues tax tables that tell you how much tax to deduct from somebody's pay for each of the weeks and months throughout the year. We won't go into the details here (your eyes may be glazing over already by now), but if we take the case of somebody with a tax allowance of £3,000 that would equate to a PAYE code of 300. During the year, at whatever payment date you were making a wages or salary payment you would look up the appropriate amount of free pay for somebody with a tax code of 300 at that moment. What you would find is that if you were paying somebody £15,000 a year each month you would pay them £1,250 gross. Of this sum, £250 is tax-free pay (you would find this in Table A of the documentation you are given by HMRC) so that you apply the tax rate of ten per cent (using Table B) to the £1,000 taxable pay. This means that you would deduct £100 from the pay each month and send that off to HMRC. At the end of the year you would have paid over £1,200.

However, you have to remember that, in addition to doing this tax calculation, you would also have to work out the National Insurance. It's quite a palaver and this is why we recommend elsewhere in the book that anybody having to cope with the rigours of PAYE and National Insurance should use a computer or get somebody else to do it for him.

What is a tax code and what is a notice of coding?

The previous question should give you an answer on your tax code. Regarding a notice of coding, anyone who is being paid through PAYE will be given one. This is a document which is sent to the taxpayer by HMRC explaining how it calculates their tax code. A much simpler document, simply giving the tax code, will be handed to the employer so that they know which tax code to apply to the employee's pay.

In other words a simple answer is – a tax code is a number given to an individual which enables the employer to work out how much tax to deduct and a notice of coding is the piece of paper on which that number has been printed by the tax authorities.

What if I fail to operate PAYE properly?

This can be very nasty. An employer who fails to operate PAYE properly can find that, when they are found out (and they will be found out!), they have to pay over not only the tax and National Insurance contributions that should have been deducted, as well as the National Insurance contributions that they, as an employer, should have been paying, but also interest on the late payment if it was paid after 19 April following the end of the tax year and a penalty of up to 100 per cent of the tax for not having done it properly in the first place.

Don't fail to operate PAYE properly.

What records does an employer have to keep?

It has often struck us as strange that there is no complete and all-embracing PAYE recording system that you can buy in a stationery shop. We ourselves have often considered devising such a system to help employers fulfil their obligations, but, to date, this has not been achieved.

A proper system for keeping employees' records would consist of the following:

For each employee:

- A contract of employment
- Notices of PAYE coding

- A permanent record sheet which would record the employees' name, date of birth, National Insurance number, date of joining, dates of pay rises, etc.

But, in addition, you would need to keep properly filed away HMRC's instructions for employers:

- Table A
- Table B
- National Insurance instructions for employers
- National Insurance tables
- Pension fund details
- … etc., etc.

In other words, an employer certainly has a number of important obligations. Our view is that, if an employer is doing their job properly, they will want to keep their records properly, pay their people properly and keep within the law. In our experience it's businesses that behave in such a manner that succeed and flourish.

What is the National Minimum Wage?

You must pay workers aged over 22 at least £5.52 per hour, rising to £5.73 in October 2008. However, there are other rates you should know, as per the following table.

	Oct 07	Oct 08
16-17 year olds	£3.40	£3.53
18-21 year olds	£4.60	£4.77
Over 21	£5.52	£5.73

HMRC is likely to ask you to prove that you are paying at least these rates, so you must keep records. Failure may result in fines of up to £5,000 for each offence.

For more information, call the Department for Business, Enterprise and Regulatory Reform (BERR) on 020 7215 5000.

What is Statutory Sick Pay and Statutory Maternity Pay?

This book is not trying to deal in depth with tax issues and the best way of finding the full answer to this particular question is to refer either to the leaflets which are handed out by HMRC to employers each year, or refer to Lawpack's book, *Employment Law Made Easy*.

However, the principle is that when someone is sick the Government expects the employer to pay that person sick pay (Statutory Sick Pay) and such payments as the employers make (up to the Statutory Sick Pay figure) can, in principle, be deducted from the National Insurance payments that are made at the end of each quarter (although large employers cannot reclaim SSP). Statutory Sick Pay is by no means generous and most employers find themselves paying more than the Statutory Sick Pay. However, the principle is that the employer makes the payment and the Government reimburses the payment (or some of it) to that employer.

In the case of Statutory Maternity Pay (SMP) (and it, too, is a complicated subject), the same principle applies, namely that the employer pays their employees who are absent to have babies and the Government reimburses the payment through the PAYE system.

What tax deductible expenses can an employee claim?

If you are an employee, which business expenses are deductible for tax purposes and which are not?

There is a general rule that any business expenses must be incurred wholly, exclusively and **necessarily** for the purposes of the business.

Clothes

Normally allowed – The cost of replacing, cleaning and repairing protective clothing (e.g. overalls, boots) and functional clothing (e.g. uniforms) necessary for your job and which you are required to provide. The cost of cleaning protective clothing or functional clothing provided by your employer, if cleaning facilities are not provided.

Not allowed – Ordinary clothes you wear for work (e.g. pinstripe suit) which you could wear outside work – even if you never choose to.

Tools, etc.

Normally allowed – The cost of maintaining and repairing tools and instruments which you are required to provide. The cost of replacing tools and instruments.

Not allowed – The initial cost of tools and instruments – but you may be able to claim capital allowances.

Cost of working at home

Normally allowed – A proportion of lighting, heating, telephone, cleaning, insurance, rent, Council Tax and water rates if part of home used exclusively for business. However, these expenses are only allowed if it's necessary that you carry out your duties at or from home (i.e. if it's an express or implied condition of your employment). Claiming Council Tax, water rates or ground rent may mean some Capital Gains Tax to pay if you sell your home – but this is unlikely.

Stationery, etc.

Normally allowed – The cost of reference books which are necessary for your job and which you are required to provide. The cost of stationery used strictly for your job.

Not allowed – The cost of books you feel you need to do your job properly but which are, in fact, unnecessary, as well as subscriptions to journals to keep up with general news.

Interest

Normally allowed – The interest on loans to buy equipment (e.g. a personal computer) necessary for the job.

Not allowed – The interest on an overdraft or credit card.

Travelling

Normally allowed – Expenses incurred strictly in the course of carrying out the job – see 'What are Authorised Mileage Payments?' on page 49. A company car: if you pay for running costs (e.g. petrol, repairs, maintenance), you can claim a proportion of the cost for business mileage.

Not allowed – Travel to and from work. The cost of buying a car.

Accompanying spouses

Normally allowed – The cost of your husband or wife travelling with you if they have, and use, a practical qualification directly associated with the trip. Often only a proportion of the cost is allowed.

Hotels and meals

Normally allowed – If you keep up a permanent home, reasonable hotel and meal expenses when travelling in the course of your job. In addition, if you stay away overnight while travelling on business, you can claim £5 for incidental expenses to cover private phonecalls, laundry and newspapers (£10 per night if you are outside the UK).

Others

Normally allowed – Pension scheme contributions. Professional subscriptions.

What is the Working Time Directive?

The Working Time Regulations came into force on 1 October 1998. Implementing a hefty chunk of the EU Social Chapter, they make big changes to the regulation of working hours.

The rules cover all workers, full-time and part-time, regardless of the size of firm for which they work and including domestic servants. They extend to quite a few who, for tax purposes, would be counted as self-employed, such as freelancers.

The regulations provide that:

1. workers don't work more than 48 hours a week;

2. night workers don't work more than eight hours a night and are offered regular health assessments;

3. workers have a rest period of 11 consecutive hours between each working day;

4. workers have an in-work rest break of 20 minutes when working more than six hours;

5. workers have at least four weeks' paid leave each year.

Only in the case of the 48-hour week may individual workers choose to agree to ignore the regulations and work more than 48 hours. If they do, the agreement must be in writing and must allow the worker to bring the agreement to an end.

There are a number of other flexibilities and a lot of detailed definitions. If you would like to learn more, you can obtain a free copy from the BERR of the *Guide to Working Time Regulations*.

What about holiday pay?

Holiday pay is not really a tax issue but it can be answered under this section.

Holiday pay would normally be dealt with in a contract of employment and all employees should be issued with a contract of employment by their employer. However, whether holiday pay is paid under a contract or under any other arrangement, it forms part of gross pay and is treated exactly the same as any other pay.

What are the rules about directors and tax?

If you are a company director and your company pays you wages, salary, bonus or commission, you must apply the PAYE procedures.

The Income Tax aspect is calculated in exactly the same way as for an employee, but there is a very important difference in the calculation of the National Insurance contributions. If you are a director, at 6 April you need to use the 'annual earnings period' calculation and if you became a director during the year you must use the 'pro-rata annual earnings period'. It's also possible for HMRC to direct that you use the 'annual earnings period' (e.g. for the spouse of a director who gets paid an annual bonus).

Further details of these methods are given on card 13 in HMRC's Employers Pack and in manual CA44, *National Insurance for Company Directors.*

What if I provide benefits for my employees?

Any benefits provided for employees must, in the first instance, be regarded as taxable and liable to be reported to HMRC.

If your employee is remunerated at a rate of less than £8,500 per year including benefits, then there are simpler reporting requirements on Form P9D. Also, not all of the benefits are taxable.

If your employee is remunerated at a rate of £8,500 or more, or is a company director (regardless of earnings), then full details must be reported on Form P11D. HMRC's booklet 480 is an invaluable guide to the whole issue of expenses and benefits payments.

The time limit for submitting Forms P9D and P11D to the Tax Office is 6 July following the tax year end. A P11D Form is reproduced at Appendix 3, for reference.

The Class 1A National Insurance contribution liability on the employer for any benefits made available to employees is calculated using the P11D information and payment must be made by 19 July.

What are Authorised Mileage Payments?

Where an employee uses their own vehicle for company purposes, they will obviously look to their employer for reimbursement for their expenses. These are now repaid using the Authorised Mileage Payment (AMP) rates, which show the maximum mileage rate that can be paid tax free.

The rates are shown in the table below and are fairly self-explanatory, but the following illustration may help.

If an employee with their own car (of whatever engine size) on which they personally pay all the expenses were to do a total of 15,000 miles in a tax year on company business, they could be paid 40p per mile for the first 10,000 miles (£4,000) and 25p per mile for the next 5,000 miles (£1,250). In total, they could be paid £5,250 tax free.

There is no requirement to show payments on an employee's Form P11D if payments are within AMP limits. If the employer pays over the limit, the excess must be declared on the P11D.

The employer should require the completion of an expense form to back up the claim that the mileage was for business purposes.

The rules are now:

Authorised Mileage Payments rates

Business mileage for 2007/08 and 2008/09	Any size of engine
Up to 10,000 miles	40p
Excess over 10,000 miles	25p

What are advisory mileage rates?

Where an employee provides the fuel for business travel in a company car, they will look to their employer for reimbursement of this expense. HMRC has published advisory mileage rates as follows:

From 1 January 2008

For petrol cars	1400cc or less	11p
	1401cc to 2000cc	13p
	over 2000cc	19p
For diesel cars	2000cc or less	11p
	over 2000cc	14p
L.P.G.	1400cc or less	7p
	1401cc to 2000cc	8p
	over 2000cc	11p

What are the rules for paying tax on motor cars provided by an employer?

This refers to tax payable by drivers of company cars. It should only concern you if you drive a company car or if you are a director of a company which provides company cars to its employees. This doesn't concern anyone who is self-employed.

With effect from 6 April 2002, the Government introduced new rules for drivers of company cars. Drivers of gas guzzlers and company car drivers who drive in excess of 18,000 miles per annum now pay much more tax. This is because Income Tax payable is assessed on the level of CO_2 emitted and the price of a new car – with no discount any longer for the age of the car or high business mileage.

So the more the CO_2 and the more expensive the car, the higher the tax bill. Company car drivers of small environmentally friendly cars, who do few business miles, are better off under the new tax regime.

The long reign of the flashy company car as king of perks is over! Such cars should either be replaced by smaller cars or be given up in favour of the equivalent salary and a car bought privately.

Every case should be judged on its merits, so look before you leap. Your company should be able to assist you with transfer of ownership, arranging favourable terms of purchase and/or finance.

What is the tax on employees' vans?

If you are an employee and are provided with a company van, before 6 April 2007 you paid tax on a standard benefit (if benefit it was) of £500 per year – or on £350 if the van was more than four years old. If the van was shared, then the taxable benefit used to be spread between the sharers. These sums were much less than the sums payable on company cars.

However, it was even better than this because if you drove a van, and even if you used it for restricted private purposes, there was no tax to pay. You could use it for going to and from work, but other private uses would create the charge. Examples of such other uses that would create a tax charge, according to HMRC, would be:

- using the van to visit the supermarket twice a week;
- taking it on holiday;
- using it for social activities.

But uses that would not trigger a tax charge included:

- taking rubbish to the tip once or twice a year;
- regularly taking a detour to the newsagent on the way to work;
- calling at the dentist on the way home.

But all that glitters is not gold. While there is now still no tax to pay if there is no, or very restricted private use, the rates have been revised since 6 April 2007. The van benefit is now £3,000 and there is a further £500 charge if fuel is provided – so beware.

Why the Chancellor taxed vans so little, then dropped all the charges, and then increased them to figures that are far more than the 2005/06 rates, defeats us!

What are the car benefit charges based on CO_2 emissions?

CO_2 emissions in grams per kilometre	Tax is based on the following percentage of the price of the car up to £80,000
2008/09	**%**
120	10
135	15*
140	16*
145	17*
150	18*
155	19*
160	20*
165	21*
170	22*
175	23*
180	24*
185	25*
190	26*
195	27*
200	28*
205	29*
210	30*
215	31*
220	32*
225	33**
230	34***
235	35****

*   add 3% if car runs solely on diesel
**   add 2% if car runs solely on diesel
***   add 1% if car runs solely on diesel
****   maximum charge so no supplement

Note: The exact CO_2 figure is rounded down to the nearest five grams per kilometre (g/km).

What are the fuel benefit charges?

Where an employer pays for the car's fuel, take the appropriate percentage from the above table and apply it to £16,900.

Can I get dispensation for travel and subsistence payments?

Most employers will have had the annual chore of having to complete the dreaded Form P11D dealing with employees' benefits.

Although it's not possible to avoid making Tax Returns for genuine benefits (including company cars), it's possible to apply for dispensation from reporting travel and subsistence payments made to employees, so long as some fairly innocuous conditions can be met (receipts are requested, expenses are incurred in the course of business, mileage rates are within HMRC's guidelines and all claims are checked by a senior employee).

How do I provide a pension scheme for my employees?

Stakeholder Pensions were introduced in April 2001 as the new low-cost private pension initiative. The Government has insisted that those employers with five or more employees must offer their staff access to a Stakeholder Pension scheme where there is no other form of company pension already in place that they would otherwise be eligible to join.

Unlike the traditional form of occupational pension, there is no legal requirement for the employer to contribute and benefits at retirement will depend on how much has been paid in, the performance of the funds while invested and the rates of interest available at retirement.

Stakeholder Pensions must meet certain standards designed to ensure they offer value for money. These standards are known as CAT (Charges, Access, Terms) standards and are summarised below:

- There is a maximum management charge of one per cent of the value of the pension fund per annum.

- The minimum contribution to the plan must be no less than £20 and the member can choose when and how often to pay.

- The plan holder must be able to switch to another scheme or pension company whenever they like and without penalty.

- Any extra benefits such as life assurance or premium protection must be optional and arranged separately from the pension plan.

Contributions are made net of basic rate Income Tax by the employee and gross where the employer decides to contribute.

Whether they offer the best value in all instances is questionable and a personal pension may be preferable where:

1. a wider choice of investment funds than is otherwise available under a Stakeholder Pension is required;

2. the charges under the personal pension are as low as or perhaps even lower than a Stakeholder Pension – perhaps where no advice is being sought or a fee is being paid to the adviser in lieu of commission.

What are the rules if I provide shares and share options for my employees?

Under the All Employee Share Ownership Plan (AESOP), employees may allocate part of their salary to shares in their employer company ('partnership shares') without paying tax or National Insurance contributions, nor are employers' National Insurance contributions payable. Employers may also give free shares to employees, including extra free shares for employees who have partnership shares ('matching shares'), and the cost of the shares and of running the scheme are tax deductible. There are maximum limits of £1,500 salary per year for partnership shares and £3,000 worth of free shares per year, although employers may set lower limits. Note: all types of share issued to employees must be reported to HMRC on Form 42 within 30 days; failure to so do means a fine of £300 per employee.

If the employee takes shares out of the scheme within five years, they are taxed under Schedule E. If the shares remain in the Scheme for five years or more, they are free of tax and National Insurance contributions when they are withdrawn.

There are two types of share option scheme: 'Save As You Earn' (SAYE)-linked share option schemes and Company Share Option Plans. Under an SAYE scheme, contributions of between £5 and £250 per month are paid under a SAYE contract with a building society or bank. The option will normally be able to be exercised after three, five or seven years when the contract ends. No charge to Income Tax arises on the difference between cost and market value when a share option is exercised, nor at the time it's granted.

The scheme enables an option to be granted now to acquire shares at today's price. The price at which the option may be exercised must not normally be less than 80 per cent of the market value of the shares at the time the option is granted.

Under approved non-savings-related share option schemes, the option must not be granted at a discount and the total market value of shares that may be acquired under the option must not exceed £30,000. If these conditions are complied with, there is no tax charge when options are granted. Nor is there a tax charge when the option is exercised, providing options under the scheme are exercised between three and ten years after they are granted, and not more frequently than once in three years.

What are the different schemes for providing shares for employees?

The different approved schemes are:

- Share Incentive Plans (SIP): Under this scheme, which is also known as an AESOP (All Employee Share Ownership Plan):

  - Employers can give up to £3,000 worth of shares to each employee.

  - Employees can buy up to £1,500 worth of shares and, under such circumstances, employers can reward the purchasers with two free shares for each share purchased.

- Savings Related Share Options Schemes (SRSOS):

  - Participants can save up to £250 per month to acquire shares at the end of a three-, five- or seven-year period.

- Enterprise Management Incentive (EMI):

  - Companies with gross assets not exceeding £30 million can grant tax and National Insurance contribution-advantaged share options worth up to £100,000 to any number of employees who work more than 25 hours per week in the business, subject to a total value of £3 million.

- Company Share Option Plans (CSOP):

  - Up to £30,000 of options each can be granted to any number of employees with tax and National Insurance contribution advantages.

- Schemes outside HMRC's approved range of schemes:

  - These will suffer tax and National Insurance contributions.

Needless to say, professional advice must be sought. For example, shares must not be issued at less than market value. In the case of unapproved schemes, the company makes up its own rules. For these, there is even more need for professional advice because if things go wrong, it can be both embarrassing and expensive.

What National Insurance is payable on employees' benefits?

If you are an employer and you complete Form P11D for any of your employees, it's likely that there will be a Class 1A National Insurance liability arising on the benefits.

The amount of Class 1A National Insurance contributions payable is calculated by reference to the value of the benefits provided and the application of the Class 1A percentage rate in force. Calculation of the Class 1A National Insurance contribution liability will be possible from the information contained in the P11D Form. Payment of the Class 1A

National Insurance contributions will be due by 19 July following the end of the year in question, i.e. 19 July 2008 for 2007/08.

Reading HMRC's booklet CWG5 is recommended and this also contains details of further sources of information.

What do employers and employees have to do at the year end?

Employer

The employer must complete Forms P14/P60, Form P35 and Forms P11D/P9D. The employer must also ensure that all payments of PAYE tax and National Insurance contributions have been paid over to the Collector of Taxes and any Class 1A National Insurance contributions due for the year will subsequently be payable. The deadlines for these various items are as follows:

Month 12 payment to the Collector of Taxes to avoid interest	19 April
Submitting the P14 and P35 to the Tax Office	19 May
Providing the P60 to your employee	31 May
Submitting Forms P11D/P9D to the Tax Office	6 July
Making the Class 1A National Insurance contributions payment to the Collector of Taxes	19 July

Employee

You should keep safely your P60. You should keep evidence of any income that you have received during the year and any tax that you have paid. This is not limited to your employment and includes all of your tax affairs as a whole.

What changes are being made to the filing of employers' End of Year Returns?

The Government believes that encouraging employers to make greater use of new technology is the best way to help them deal with their payroll tasks.

As part of the measures to support this change, all employers will be required to file their End of Year Returns electronically by 2010. The compulsory electronic filing date depends on the number of employees an employer has.

Number of employees	First compulsory electronic Return	Filing deadline
250 or more	2004/05 year end	19 May 2005
Between 50 and 249	2005/06 year end	19 May 2006
Fewer than 50	2009/10 year end	19 May 2010

There are financial incentives for employers with fewer than 50 employees who make the transition from paper to e-filing earlier. All qualifying employers who successfully e-file for these years are entitled to the payment shown below, including those already e-filing.

End of Year Return	2007/08	2008/09
Incentive £	100	75

These payments are even more of an incentive to use a computer to cope with PAYE or to get someone else, such as your accountant, to do it for you. Either way, the cash incentive is available.

What are the rules for charitable giving through the PAYE system?

If an employer participates in the Payroll Giving scheme, an employee can authorise the deduction of whatever sum they choose from their earnings before tax, for passing on to charities chosen by them, through a charity agency with which the employer has made an arrangement. The employee thus receives full tax relief for the contributions made.

What tax is payable on payments for compensation for loss of office?

Compensation for loss of office and wages in lieu of notice are both taxable when provided for in the terms and conditions of the employment. Also, if the payment is of deferred earnings, this, too, is taxable under the normal PAYE rules.

Provided that the payment is not caught by the normal PAYE rules, the first £30,000 of the redundancy payment is exempt from tax. Any surplus received over and above this is treated as earnings and PAYE applied in the normal way.

Statutory redundancy payments, while not taxable in themselves, are included within the £30,000 exemption.

Payments for death or disability in service are not taxable. Lump sums received under approved pension schemes are also exempt from tax.

What are the tax rules if I'm employed outside the UK?

If your employment abroad is full-time, spans a complete tax year and you actually carry out all your duties abroad, you are normally treated by concession as a non-resident from the date of leaving until the date of return. If you don't attain non-resident status, you will therefore be a UK resident throughout.

If you visit the UK, to retain non-resident status your visits must not add up to 183 days in any tax year, or average 91 days per tax year over a four-year period. Overstepping these limits will result in you being treated as resident and ordinarily resident in the UK.

The benefit of attaining non-resident status is that you escape UK tax on all of your earnings abroad. You may find Appendix 8 helpful.

What are 'fixed deductions'?

These are flat rate expenses for employees to cover the cost of tools, special clothing, etc. not provided by their employer. The amounts are mostly agreed with trade unions and don't preclude further claims, if justified. For further information, contact your local Tax Office.

CHAPTER 5

Pensions and tax

What is pensions simplification?

On 6 April 2006 ('A-Day'), new simplified rules came into effect concerning how pensions are taxed, offering simpler and more flexible retirement arrangements. Here is an outline of the changes:

1. The many existing set of rules governing the taxation of pensions were replaced with a single, universal regime.

2. For the first time, everyone could save in more than one pension scheme at the same time.

3. There is no limit on the amount of money you can save in a pension scheme or the number of pension schemes you can save in – although there are some limits on the amount of tax relief you can get.

4. You will get tax relief on contributions up to 100 per cent of your annual earnings (up to an annual allowance set at £235,000 in 2008/09). So if you put £100 into your pension scheme, the tax relief the Government gives you on this amount is worth at least £25.

5. Even if you are not a taxpayer, you can still get tax relief on pension contributions. You can put in up to £2,880 in any one tax year and the Government will top this up with another £720 – giving you total pension savings with tax relief of £3,600 per year.

6. A-Day introduces flexible retirement, allowing people in occupational pension schemes to continue working while drawing their pension, where the scheme rules allow it.

7. If your scheme rules allow, you can take up to 25 per cent of your pension fund as a tax-free lump sum.

8. If your pension pot is more than the 'Lifetime Allowance' when you come to take your pension, you may be subject to a tax charge at that time. But this will only apply if your total pension savings are in excess of £1.65 million from 6 April 2008 (rising to £1.8 million by 2010/11 and reviewed thereafter).

9. Those individuals with larger pensions pots at A-Day are able to protect their funds from the Lifetime Allowance Charge by completing and submitting the appropriate form to HM Revenue & Customs (HMRC). They have three years from A-Day to do this, i.e. until 5 April 2009.

10. The rules on when you can take your pension have changed. From 6 April 2010 you won't be able to take a pension before you are 55. There are a couple of exceptions: you will still be able to retire early due to poor health, and if you have the right to retire before 50 at 6 April 2006, that right may be protected.

Is it worth paying into a pension scheme?

Now here is a very interesting question. Over the years of our being in practice, we have discovered that clients save towards their retirement in a number of different ways. Some don't wish to pay into a pension scheme, preferring to invest on their own, either through property or other types of clever investment. This route doesn't suit everyone and we would encourage our clients to make sure that they are fully aware of the associated risks before pursuing such a strategy.

For many, the discipline of saving on a regular basis for their retirement appeals with the attraction of tax relief on contributions and the virtually tax-free growth that can be enjoyed while their money is invested.

Whichever route our clients take, there are obviously charges to consider. For pensions this could be commission and/or fees paid to an adviser, while for property purchase it might be legal fees such as Stamp Duty, solicitors' costs, etc.

What are SIPPs?

SIPPs are Self Invested Personal Pensions and they allow individuals direct control over the investments in their pension scheme. They provide maximum flexibility in the timing of contributions into, and benefit payments from, the scheme.

An example of such flexibility is that a SIPP allows for up to 25 per cent of the fund to be withdrawn tax free between the ages of 55 and 75. The balance then can be used to provide income for the rest of the individual's life.

SIPPs also provide an attraction for Inheritance Tax purposes because if the individual dies before retirement, the whole of the value of the SIPP is excluded from the deceased's estate.

There are many assets that can be included in a SIPP but some are specifically excluded (e.g. residential property, works of art, fine wines and vintage cars).

One advantage of a SIPP is the opportunity it provides for investing in smaller companies. Another is that a SIPP can borrow up to 50 per cent of its value.

Some individuals who invest in a SIPP, opt for the management to be handled at the discretion of an investment management company. One advantage of this is the clear reporting and administrative package that usually comes with such management.

The SIPP market is growing.

What sort of state pension can I expect?

If you ring up the Pension Service (tel. 0845 300 0168) giving it your National Insurance number, it should be able to send you a forecast of your anticipated state pension at retirement which it will work out based on your age and contributions to date.

CHAPTER 6

Self-employment and partnerships

Should I tell the taxman if I'm going self-employed or starting a partnership?

When you begin self-employment it's very important that somebody (you or your accountant) tells HM Revenue & Customs (HMRC) that you have begun in business, partly so that the correct tax can be paid on time and partly so that the appropriate National Insurance contributions are paid. Anyone beginning self-employment or a partnership must register with HMRC within three months from the end of the month in which the self-employment commenced. Failure to meet this deadline can result in a £100 penalty.

There are two forms which you should complete for the tax authorities, 'CWF1 Notification of Self-Employment' and 'CA5601 Application to Pay Class 2 Contributions by Direct Debit', obtainable from any HMRC office or from the HMRC website (at www.hmrc.gov.uk). Do bear in mind that if your profits or share of profits for 2008/09 are below £4,825 you may claim exemption from paying Class 2 contributions. As we have said before (on page 29), this is only sensible if you have other earnings on which you are paying contributions.

Self-employment worries can be taken care of (and avoided) if you choose an accountant to handle your accounts and to advise you about the resulting tax liabilities.

What is trading?

It's sometimes difficult to know if an activity is taxable or not. Typical (in other words difficult) questions might be as follows:

- If I earn £300 a year from self-employed activities does the taxman want to know?

- My daughter, who is still at school, earns £50 a week from singing in local pubs; does the taxman want to know?

- I occasionally do small jobs for people, being paid in cash; will the taxman want to know?

It's always difficult to give the right answer because, while we know that under law if you are earning money the taxman will want to know, even if there is no tax to be paid, there is that famous maxim, which we cover elsewhere in this book, 'de minimis non curat lex', which means 'the law is not concerned with trifles'.

Trading is earning money from an activity. Trading involves not only the earning of the money but also the expenses in achieving that income. Our advice to clients is: use the template we show in Appendix 4 and see if you have made a taxable sum from the activity. If you have, you should report it. Your conscience will tell you if you should be reporting it.

When an activity is in the grey area of being between non-reportable and reportable, each case has to be taken on its merits and decisions arrived at accordingly. However, in principle, once one is trading (earning money from an activity) proper records should be kept and HMRC should be told.

How do I calculate my taxable income from trading?

Basically, you have to take your income and deduct from it all your legitimate business-related expenses. You will see the type of expenses that you can claim in Appendix 4 and you will see these listed in more detail below. However, do bear in mind that some expenses, for instance motoring, may well involve an element of private use. You should only claim that element that relates to the business activity against your trading receipts. It may be that you should only claim a third of your motoring costs against your business. Perhaps a quarter of your Council Tax and insurance costs. Whatever it is, if you have any difficulties in deciding, either go and see a local accountant or visit the Tax Office to discuss it.

A template to help you prepare your figures for the self-employed part of the Tax Return is provided at Appendix 4.

What expenses can I claim?

There is a general rule that any business expenses must be incurred wholly and exclusively for the purposes of the business. This means that some expenses will fall foul of the so-called dual purpose rule. For example, if you attend a business conference in Spain and tack a holiday on the end, your trip will have a dual purpose and the expenses won't be allowed. However, according to HMRC, 'in practice some dual purpose expenses include an obvious part which is for the purposes of the business. We usually allow the deduction of a proportion of expenses like that', and they go on to give the example of car or van expenses.

Basic costs and general running expenses

Normally allowed – The cost of goods bought for resale and raw materials used in business. Advertising, delivery charges, heating, lighting, cleaning, rates, telephone. The rent of business premises. The replacement of small tools and special clothing. Postage, stationery, relevant books and magazines. Accountants' fees. Bank charges on business accounts. Fees to professional bodies. Security expenditure.

Not allowed – The initial cost of machinery, vehicles, equipment, permanent advertising signs in excess of £50,000 – but you can claim capital allowances. The cost of buildings. Providing for anticipated expenses in the future.

Use of home for work

Normally allowed – The business proportion of telephone calls and line rental, lighting, heating, cleaning, insurance, rent, Council Tax and mortgage interest. Provided you don't use any part of your home exclusively for business purposes, you won't lose your entitlement to private residence relief for Capital Gains Tax.

Wages and salaries

Normally allowed – Wages, salaries, redundancy and leaving payments paid to employees. Pensions for past employees and their dependants. Staff training.

Not allowed – Your own wages or salary or that of any business partner. Your own drawings.

Tax and National Insurance

Normally allowed – Employer's National Insurance contributions for employees. Reasonable pay for your spouse, provided they are actually employed.

Not allowed – Income Tax. Capital Gains Tax. Inheritance Tax. Your own National Insurance contributions.

Entertaining

Normally allowed – Entertainment of own staff (e.g. a Christmas party).

Not allowed – Any other business entertaining.

Pre-trading

Normally allowed – Revenue business expenditure incurred within seven years before starting to trade.

Gifts

Normally allowed – Gifts costing up to £50 a year to each person so long as the gift advertises your business (or things it sells). Gifts (whatever their value) to employees.

Not allowed – Food, drink, tobacco or vouchers for goods given to anyone other than employees.

Travelling

Normally allowed – Hotel and travelling expenses on business trips. Travel between different places of work. The running costs of your own car – whole of cost if used wholly for business, proportion if used privately too.

Not allowed – Travel between home and business. The cost of buying a car or van (but you can claim capital allowances).

If a business leases a car costing more than £12,000, part of the leasing cost is disallowed for tax purposes. The rules are complicated but, in principle, the more expensive the car you lease, the smaller the proportion that you will be allowed to claim as a tax deduction in your accounts.

Interest payments

Normally allowed – The interest on overdrafts and loans for business purposes.

Not allowed – The interest on capital paid or credited to partners.

Hire purchase

Normally allowed – Hire charge part of instalments (i.e. the amount you pay less the cash price). There is a restriction if the interest relates to a car purchase in excess of £12,000.

Not allowed – Cash price of what you are buying on hire purchase (but you may get capital allowances).

Hiring

Normally allowed – Reasonable charge for hire of capital goods, including cars.

Insurance

Normally allowed – Business insurance (e.g. employer's liability, fire and theft, motor, insuring employees' lives).

Not allowed – Your own life insurance.

Trade marks

Normally allowed – Fees paid to register a trademark, design or patent.

Not allowed – The cost of buying a patent from someone else (but you may get capital allowances).

Legal costs

Normally allowed – The costs of recovering debts, defending business rights, preparing service agreements, appealing against rates, renewing a lease for a period not exceeding 50 years (but not if a premium is paid).

Not allowed – Expenses (including Stamp Duty) for acquiring land, buildings or leases. Fines and other penalties for breaking the law.

Repairs

Normally allowed – Normal repairs and maintenance to premises or equipment.

Not allowed – The cost of additions, alterations, improvements (but you may get capital allowances).

Debts

Normally allowed – Specific provisions for debts and debts written off.

Not allowed – General reserve for bad or doubtful debts.

Subscriptions

Normally allowed – Payments which secure benefits for your business or staff. Payments to societies that have arrangements with HMRC (in some cases only a proportion).

Not allowed – Payments to political parties, churches and charities (but small gifts to local churches and charities may be allowed).

Travelling and subsistence expenses and tax

Expenses	Employer	Self-employed	Can VAT (Input Tax) be reclaimed?
	Where expenses are incurred by the employer, whether a self-employed trader, a partnership or a company	Where a self-employed trader incurs these expenses on his own behalf	
Entertaining own staff	Allowable	Allowable	Yes*
Business travel between place of business and customers, etc. (but not home)	Allowable	Allowable	Yes
Hotel bills, etc.	Allowable	Allowable	Yes, so long as it's billed to the VAT-registered trader

Drinks and meals away from home:			
1. Working/ selling	Allowable	Not allowable	Yes*
2. On training course	Allowable	Allowable	Yes*
3. Buying, trips etc.	Allowable	Allowable	Yes*
Entertaining business clients	Not allowable	Not allowable	No
Car parking	Allowable	Allowable	Yes
Trade show expenses	Allowable	Allowable	Yes
Fuel	Allowable	Allowable (business proportion only)	Yes**

*	But not if there is any measurable degree of Business Entertainment.
**	But if the input VAT is reclaimed, remember to include the scale charge in your OUTPUT TAX on the VAT Return.

Can I pay myself?

The answer to this is no. If you look at this logically you will see how the answer can only be no. If you were to pay yourself a salary out of your self-employment or partnership income you would have to include the salary as employment income elsewhere on your Tax Return and thereby you would achieve nothing.

Under this section you could also consider whether you could pay your spouse. If they play a part in the business and have no other income, then there might well be tax to save by paying them for the work that they do.

What is the tax significance of holding trading stock?

If you are running a business that involves the buying and selling of items of stock, at the end of your trading year you have to add up the cost of any unsold stock and deduct it from the cost of your purchases acquired during the year. The reason for this is that those stocks are going to be sold in the following accounting period and therefore you only take advantage of the tax relief that goes with buying those stocks in the year or period in which they are sold. In other words any stocks that you deduct from your cost of sales at the end of your trading period should be added to the costs that you incur in the following year, so that you claim the deduction in the correct year. If you think that your stock may not sell for what you paid for it or it's slow moving, you can write it down to what is called 'net realisable value'.

What is the tax significance of work in progress?

If you have been working on a long contract, the duration of which straddles the end of your accounting period, you are likely to have incurred costs in terms of labour and materials at the end of your year which relate to that contract and which you have not been paid for. Accordingly, you should value those materials, as well as those hours and, as with stocks, carry the sum forward to the following year so as to take advantage of those costs in the year in which you bill your customer for the work. If you have reached a point where you are entitled to be paid for the work done, then part of the work in progress will have to be valued at selling price, not at cost. This is a complicated area and we do recommend that you take advice from either the taxman or a local accountant.

Do remember that, in assessing the value of work in progress, if you are a partner or a sole proprietor in a business, you don't need to include your own time. However, you do need to include materials.

What are debtors and what do I do about them?

Debtors are sums owed to you by your customers, but which have not been paid at the end of your accounting period. Even though you have not been paid you do have to include these as amounts due to you. If any of them have subsequently proved to be bad or look doubtful (i.e. you are not going to be paid or you may not be paid), you can claim as an expense a figure relating specifically to the ones that are not going to be, or may not be, paid.

Come the next accounting period, and when that cash comes in, you don't pay tax on that money, because it has already been taxed in the previous year.

What are creditors and what do I do about them?

Creditors are like debtors but the other way round: they are the sums that you owe that you have not paid by the end of your financial year. You are allowed to include these sums in your accounts, and get the tax relief for them in the year to which they relate. However, when you come to pay them in the following year, you won't be entitled to tax relief in that year because you have already got the tax relief in the previous year.

What are capital allowances and agricultural and industrial buildings allowances?

You are unable to claim the depreciation charged in your accounts as a tax deduction. Instead, you have to claim, and in a prescribed way, HMRC's own version of depreciation which it calls 'capital allowances'. These also include agricultural and industrial buildings allowances. You will almost certainly need professional help to do this properly. These allowances are specifically allowed as a deduction against your taxable profits. In the year starting 6 April 2008, you can claim capital allowances as follows:

	First-year allowance % that can be claimed by any business	Writing down allowance % of balance that can be claimed
Plant	nil	20%
Machinery	nil	20%
Vans	nil	20%

Patents	nil	20%
Know-how	nil	20%
Information & Communications Technology	nil	20%
Computers	nil	20%
Digital TV	nil	20%
Websites	nil	20%
Energy-saving and water-saving plant & machinery	100%	Nil
Most cars	Nil	20%*
Some cars with low carbon dioxide emissions (see Appendix 13)	100%	Nil
Industrial buildings	Nil (100% in Enterprise Zone)	3% (25% in Enterprise Zone)
Agricultural buildings	Nil	3%

* There are proposals to reduce this to 10% from 6 April 2009 for cars with CO_2 emissions above 160gm/km.

What is the Annual Investment Allowance?

This is a new allowance applicable from April 2008. Expenditure of up to £50,000 per annum on plant, machinery, long life assets and integral features will be relieved **in full** against profits. Any expenditure above this limit will be relieved using the normal capital allowance rules. Where an accounting period spans 1 April for companies, or 6 April for individuals, this allowance is reduced pro rata. Similarly, accounting periods which are less than, or greater than, 12 months will also get a reduced allowance.

From 1 April 2008 (for companies) or 6 April 2008 (for individuals), where the written down value of the plant and machinery pool is £1,000 or less, this can be written off in full if desired. These two changes taken together mean that many small businesses – especially those which are labour rather than capital intensive, as are many service businesses – will be able to claim 100 per cent of their capital expenditure in the year in which they make it. This is a useful and worthwhile simplification.

What are long life assets and what allowances do they get?

Long life assets are items of plant or machinery which are expected to last at least 25 years. The writing down allowance for them is increased from six per cent to ten per cent. A new 'pool' is created to include long life assets and integral features.

As a consequence of the changes in the rates applicable to the different pools, a 'hybrid rate' of capital allowances has to be calculated when the accounting period spans 1 April (companies) or 6 April (individuals). For example, with an accounting period covering 1 January 2008 to 31 December 2008, the hybrid rate of capital allowances would be:

91/366 x 25%	=	6.22%
275/366 x 20%	=	15.03%
Hybrid rate for the transitional period	=	21.25%

Can loss-making companies claim cash back in lieu of their capital allowances?

Where a limited company incurs expenditure on or after 1 April 2008 on energy-saving or environmentally-friendly plant and machinery which is eligible for 100 per cent capital allowances, if the company is making a loss, then the loss arising from the expenditure can be surrendered for a cash payment from the Government. The company will receive a 19 per cent tax credit on the loss surrendered up to a maximum of the higher of (a) the total of the company's PAYE and NIC liabilities for the period of the loss, or (b) £250,000.

Is there any special tax treatment for farmers?

There are two specific ways in which farmers get special tax treatment:

1. **The herd basis.** In recent years, this has been less of an attraction as a means of saving tax because the value of farm animals has fallen during this period. However, the principle of the herd basis is that, because a herd, or a flock for that matter, consists of breeding animals (cows, bulls, rams, ewes), instead of treating these as animals that you will ultimately sell as meat, you treat them as capital assets and not as a revenue item. This book on tax is not the place to describe this particular feature but the effect of claiming the herd basis at a time of rising animal values is that, when you come to sell those animals (perhaps retire), a substantial part of the sale proceeds won't be subject to tax.

   How should farmers value their stocks? Farm stocks and farm animals that are not part of a herd or flock should be valued at the lower of cost or net realisable value. In a number of cases 'cost' will be easy to calculate, but what about animals that have grown considerably since they were bought, animals that have been home bred and crops? For such stocks where it's just not possible to calculate an appropriate 'cost' figure, HMRC allows farmers to use a percentage of market value at the valuation date. These are:

   - Cattle: 60%

   - Sheep and pigs: 75%

   - Deadstock: 75%

2. **Averaging.** Because farm results can fluctuate, farmers are able to claim the averaging of profits of any pair of consecutive years of assessment provided they do so within broadly 22 months of the end of the second year. As with the herd basis, the rules can be quite complicated, but the effect of claiming for averaging is that you can collectively pay less tax than you would if you had a very high profit attracting higher rates of tax in one year and a loss or lower profits in the adjacent year.

Is there any special tax treatment for visiting sports stars and entertainers?

The bad news is that UK appearances by non-resident sportspeople and entertainers are taxed at once. Payments of £1,000 or more are subject to basic rate Income Tax at source. The good news is that it's possible to agree a lower or nil rate with HMRC where it can be established that the eventual United Kingdom tax liability will be less than basic rate.

Is there any special tax treatment for Lloyd's insurance underwriters?

Yes, there is special treatment for Lloyd's underwriters. It's such a complicated set of rules, allowances and regulations that our advice is to say, as succinctly as possible, go to a specialist adviser who deals with Lloyd's underwriters.

Is there any special tax treatment for subcontractors?

Construction Industry Scheme – the new rules

The new system for those working in the construction industry came into force on 6 April 2007. There are four major changes:

1. Registration cards and certificates are replaced by a verification process which determines whether subcontractors should be paid gross or net. Subcontractors applying for registration have to prove their identity to HMRC, who then register the applicant for payment under deduction at the 18 per cent rate. Those registering for gross payment have to satisfy three further tests – much the same as under the old system. These tests are as follows:

   (a) Turnover test – you must have a net turnover, i.e. sales less cost of materials, of at least £30,000, in three of the last four years. For partnerships the net turnover figure of £30,000 is multiplied by the number of partners. For a new business, you must have a total turnover of £21,000 in any six consecutive months leading up to the date of application.

(b) Compliance test – you must have kept your tax affairs up to date for one year, including paying your tax and National Insurance on time and always operating the construction industry scheme correctly. If you have incurred any tax penalties you are likely to fail this test.

(c) Business test – you must own your own stocks. You must own your own equipment. You must keep proper books of account and you must operate from proper business premises.

2. Contractors have to make monthly returns and provide monthly statements of amounts paid. Contractors have 14 days to send in the returns and make payment (17 days if the payment is made electronically) and nil returns have to be submitted.

3. The contractor has to declare that they consider the subcontractor to be self-employed. This is always a difficult area and the questionnaire on pages 37–40 may be a useful starting point.

4. There is a new 30 per cent rate of deduction which is to be used for those who are not registered.

Under the transitional rules existing gross and net payee status carry on as before. So registration only applies to new subcontractors or to those wishing to move from net payment to gross payment.

Contractors would be well advised to have suitable software in place to cope with the monthly returns and paperwork. Penalties range from £100 up to £3,000.

Is there any special tax treatment for owners of mineral rights and royalties?

If you receive income from mineral rights or you are an author or composer by profession, then your receipts are taxed as part of your professional earnings and you are able to deduct more expenses than otherwise would be the case. In principle, you pay tax in the year in which the mineral rights or royalties are received, but there are rules for spreading royalty receipts over a number of years and, should you fall within this case, we strongly advise you to seek professional advice.

How do I get tax relief for losses in my business?

Trading losses may be:

1. relieved against income or gains of the same year;

2. relieved against income or gains of the previous year;

3. carried forward against future profits of the same trade.

In the case of both points 1 and 2, you must claim the full loss, up to the total income for that year. From 6 April 2008, for individuals carrying on a trade in a non-active capacity, i.e. spending on average less than ten hours per week on the commercial activities of the trade, there is an annual limit of £25,000 for losses which can be set against other income in the year.

Are there any special rules about claiming farm losses?

Because a number of wealthy people used to claim the substantial losses they made through their farming activities against their other substantial income, HMRC said that it would limit the number of years for which someone in this category could go on claiming farming losses.

How many years of farm losses can one utilise before having to carry forward those losses?

Five. A loss in the sixth tax year of a consecutive run of farming losses can only be relieved against later profits of the same trade. Once you have made a farming profit then the five-year sequence starts again.

The figure of loss or profit is arrived at before claiming capital allowances.

HMRC allows stud farms to incur losses for 11 years.

What is Class 4 National Insurance?

If you are trading and your profits exceed £5,435, you have to pay eight per cent Class 4 National Insurance contributions on the figure of your profits above £5,435 with an annual upper earnings limit of £40,040. Above this upper earnings limit, you have to pay one per cent on all profits above this figure.

What is a partnership?

A partnership is a formal business arrangement entered into by two or more people whereby the profits and losses of a business are shared in agreed proportions.

In order for HMRC to be happy that a partnership exists, it may want to see a number of the following items before it will agree to tax the business as a partnership:

- A partnership deed.

- The names of partners on bank statements.

- The names of partners on business letterheadings and other printed stationery.

- Some sort of evidence that the parties agreed that there should be a formal partnership between them.

The Government has introduced new rules to restrict losses made by 'non-active' partners in the first four years. If the loss is to be claimed against other income or gain, it will be restricted to the capital contribution made, unless you work more than ten hours a week for the partnership.

Should I go into partnership with my spouse?

We are slow to encourage spouses to go into partnership with each other. The reason for this is that it's important for any partnership to be a genuine one (and not simply a tax dodge – because those don't work). If there is a partnership, there has to be due recognition given to the fact that there are certain legal obligations which go with being a partner. In most cases, it's not wise for a family to put this sort of working straitjacket around their family relationship.

Obvious cases where husband and wife partnerships should exist are where they both share equally in the work and it's only right and proper that they should be partners. However, in general, we don't think husband/wife partnerships are a good idea and the main legal disadvantages in having such partnerships are that:

- both partners become jointly and severally liable for the partnership debts and this can put the family home at risk;

- in the case of divorce, the 'busting' of the partnership can result in the complete cessation of the business.

Where there is a bona fide husband/wife partnership, the following documentation should be available to prove to HMRC the existence of the partnership:

1. There should be a letter issued to all customers of the business stating the appointment of a new partner and the date of the appointment.

2. There should be a written partnership agreement. If it's to be a bona fide partnership agreement, this should be prepared by a solicitor.

3. The names of the partners should appear on the letterheads and invoices, etc. of the business.

4. The names of the partners should appear on the business bank account.

5. The names of the partners should appear in the advertising and promotional literature.

6. If the business is VAT-registered, then it should be registered as a partnership with both the names of the partners on the VAT Return.

7. There should be a Notice of Particulars of Ownership displayed at the business's main centre so that any casual caller will see that there is a partnership in existence.

Do I need to have a partnership deed?

Our advice to any partners is that there should be a partnership deed so that, if anything should happen to one of the partners, or they should fall out, there is a legal agreement entered into at the start which establishes how the partnership should be dissolved and how the assets and liabilities allocated.

Perhaps, where there is a partnership between husband and wife (and this is often not a good idea for a great number of reasons), it's not that essential to have a partnership deed, but in every other case that we have come across we have always recommended that the parties go to a solicitor and draw up a proper partnership deed. Alternatively, Lawpack publishes a Partnership Agreement (F211).

What are limited liability partnerships?

The Act creating this corporate business vehicle, the limited liability partnership (LLP), allows organisations the flexibility to enjoy limited liability while organising themselves (sharing profits, etc.) as partnerships. The LLP is a separate legal entity. It's governed by agreement between the members (an incorporation document). Nevertheless, it's required to disclose, to Companies House, similar information to that required of companies. It is, however, taxed as a partnership.

We look on this structure with some interest because we regard the limitation of liability as being more theoretical than real. When companies fail, in our experience, the directors often have to pay up on previously given guarantees and if the company has failed through maladministration, then directors and quasi-directors can be sued as private individuals.

In principle, we think LLPs are a good thing, but in practice we don't think it has made much difference to anybody. Few LLPs have been registered and they are mainly large professional firms.

What happens if partners change?

If partners change, when the partnership Tax Return is completed and the ratio of agreed profits or losses for the year in question is allocated to the varying partners (whether static, incoming or outgoing), that share is shown clearly on the partnership Tax Return and the individual partners themselves pay the tax that their share attracts.

How are partnerships taxed?

Partnerships have their own Tax Return. The accounts are entered into the relevant boxes on the partnership Tax Return and the profits or losses are allocated between the partners in the agreed proportions.

In addition, the partnership must prepare individual sheets called either 'Partnership (Short)' or 'Partnership (Long)' depending on the nature of the income that the partnership earns, and these individual sheets are handed to the partners themselves for attaching to their own individual personal Tax Returns.

In other words, partnerships don't pay tax. It's the partners who pay tax on their share of the profits.

What happens about partnership capital gains?

If a partnership makes a capital gain it's included on the partnership Tax Return and the share of the capital gains must be added to the individual partner's personal Tax Returns so that each pays tax on their share of the gain.

How long do I have to keep my accounting records?

There is a legal requirement to keep accounting records for six years.

How might HM Revenue & Customs inquire into my tax affairs?

HM Revenue & Customs (HMRC) is entitled to investigate for one of three reasons; either:

1. it thinks a minor point is wrong and needs to be corrected (an 'aspect' enquiry); or

2. it doesn't like the look of the accounts and suspects that there may be something fundamentally wrong (a 'full' enquiry); or

3. the nasty bit, a Tax Return may be selected at random.

When a letter arrives from the Inspector of Taxes, you can't tell what has triggered the process. So just because your accounts may be investigated, don't get worried. Sooner or later everyone will have an investigation.

CHAPTER 7

Income from land and property

What is the wear-and-tear allowance?

This applies to furnished lettings only. It's normal for taxpayers in receipt of income from land and property to claim all their allowable expenses (see Appendix 6 for a template for identifying those expenses) against income. However, instead of claiming for the cost of renewing furniture, furnishings and fixtures such as cookers, dishwashers or washing machines, taxpayers are entitled to charge a ten per cent wear-and-tear allowance instead. This ten per cent allowance is calculated as being ten per cent of rent received, less Council Tax and water rates paid (see below).

It may be better to claim actual cost – but only when you replace the item – so we do urge taxpayers to keep proper records of all expenditure incurred in connection with their land and property income.

How do I claim losses from land and property?

There is a difference between the tax treatment of a land and property loss and a trading loss. Losses from land and property income can only be carried forward and set against profits in subsequent years from land and property.

The only exception to this is if you have any losses on furnished holiday lettings; as that is treated as a trade, you may offset such losses against your other income or capital gains in the same year or the previous one.

What is the difference between furnished lettings and furnished holiday lettings?

Furnished lettings

If you receive income from furnished lettings, it's taxed under the property income rules.

If you provide laundry, meals, domestic help, etc. for your tenants, then you may be able to claim that you are running a self-employed business – as you usually can if you are providing holiday lettings (see below). The advantage of running your property enterprise as a trading business means that there are usually more expenses you can claim against Income Tax and, in addition, you may be able to claim entrepreneurs' relief for Capital Gains Tax and business property relief for Inheritance Tax purposes.

Furnished holiday lettings

If you let out holiday accommodation, the definition of furnished holiday lettings is as follows:

* The accommodation must be available for holiday lets for at least 140 days per year.
* The accommodation must be let for 70 days in the year.
* No let to exceed 31 days.

The income is treated as earned income (a trade) attracting Capital Gains Tax rollover relief and entrepreneurs' relief.

Tax-saving ideas worth thinking about...

* Rollover of capital gains on the sale of trading assets into the purchase of holiday accommodation.

- Any gain on the sale of the holiday accommodation may eventually attract Capital Gains Tax at only ten per cent. (See page 102 for the Government's recent changes to Capital Gains Tax.)

- You can claim capital allowances on furniture and equipment.

- If you make a trading loss from your holiday lets you may offset it against your other income or capital gains in the same year or the previous one.

However...

- Don't buy the accommodation with a substantial mortgage because the HM Revenue & Customs (HMRC) may regard your motives as not being commercial.

- Don't forget about the VAT consequences, if you are VAT-registered.

What is rent-a-room relief?

If you let a room in your house and you are an owner-occupier, or a tenant who is sub-letting, the first £4,250 of any income is tax free, i.e. a rent of £81.73 per week is tax free.

If the rent is higher than £4,250, you either elect to pay tax on the surplus above £4,250 (without relief for expenses) or you can treat the arrangement as being a furnished letting and prepare accounts.

This relief is available whether you rent out just one room to a lodger or you run a bed & breakfast business from your house.

Woodlands – what are the rules about selling timber?

There is no Income Tax charge on woodlands; neither woodland rent nor the sale of timber is taxed. There is no charge to Capital Gains Tax on trees that are standing or felled. In other words, proceeds of sale of timber are not taxed at all.

How are property developers taxed?

You may find, perhaps because you are a developer, that you carry out a number of purchases and sales of land and buildings and that, instead of these transactions being treated as falling within the Capital Gains Tax regime, the profits and losses you make are caught under the Income Tax regime. There are some taxpayers who have been badly caught by this and in principle it's quite difficult to give a hard-and-fast rule as to when somebody moves from the Capital Gains Tax regime to the Income Tax regime. However, all may not be lost, because when a capital asset falls within the Income Tax regime, not only are the losses more favourably treated, but also there are usually more expenses that can be claimed as well.

In our opinion, you should seek professional advice if this eventuality comes to pass in your case.

What is the tax wheeze for buy-to-let investors?

There is an interesting addition to HMRC's manuals which indicates that interest on funds borrowed for private purposes may be deductible against rental income in certain circumstances. This has wide-reaching implications for buy-to-let investors.

One example in the manual covers Mr A who owns a flat in London and is moving abroad. He decides to let the property while he is away. During his period of ownership, the property has trebled in value. He renegotiates the mortgage to convert it to a buy-to-let mortgage and borrows a further amount which he uses to buy a property overseas. Can he claim tax relief on the interest against the rents? Well, HMRC says that owners of businesses (and renting property is a business for tax purposes) are entitled to withdraw their capital from the business, even though substitute funding then has to be provided by interest-bearing loans. In the case of Mr A, his opening balance sheet shows the following:

Original mortgage	80,000	**Property at market value**	375,000
Capital account	295,000		
	£375,000		£375,000

When Mr A renegotiates his mortgage, he borrows a further £125,000 which goes through his property business. He then withdraws this amount to fund the purchase of the property overseas. By the end of the first year of letting, his balance sheet shows the following.

Mortgage	205,000	**Property at market value**	375,000
Capital account b/f	295,000		
Less drawings	(125,000)		
Carry forward	170,000		
	£375,000		£375,000

Although he has withdrawn capital from the business, the interest on the mortgage loan is allowable in full because it's funding the transfer of the property to the business at its open market value at the time the business started. Although HMRC's example has a further mortgage of £125,000, it seems that Mr A could withdraw a further £170,000 of tax-allowable finance. However, he should not take out more than he puts in as his capital account will be in the red (i.e. overdrawn).

The best advice is not to assume that you will automatically get tax relief but to take professional advice before you remortgage.

What is the difference between people owning property as joint tenants and as tenants in common?

While it may seem strange to refer to property owners as being tenants, those owning it as joint tenants own the property in equal shares. Those owning it as tenants in common, own it in a nominated or chosen proportion which need not be equal.

One consequence of owning property as joint tenants is that on the death of one, their share passes automatically to the survivor. If the property is owned as tenants in common, on death the share doesn't pass automatically to the other owner.

How are lease premiums taxed?

Lease premiums are now becoming 'more a thing of the past', but if you do grant a lease of not more than 50 years' duration, for which you receive a premium, then you will be assessed for Income Tax on the premium. The taxable amount is quite complicated to calculate but (putting a block of ice on your head we will try to explain it): you take the premium and reduce it by 1/50th of its amount for each complete period of 12 months, other than the first 12 months, and this amount is subject to Income Tax. The balance of the premium is normally subject to Capital Gains Tax.

What are the rules for leases and Stamp Duty?

These are complicated so you should seek professional advice. In effect, if you take out a lease you are likely to have to pay Stamp Duty Land Tax (see page 148 for more information).

CHAPTER 8

Income from dividends and interest

How are dividends taxed and can I claim the tax back?

The means of taxing dividends from shares has changed since 6 April 1999. Before that date it was possible, under the right circumstances, to claim a refund of the tax deducted on the dividend. Now that is no longer possible.

The new rules are somewhat complex: the old rate of tax on dividends of 20 per cent has now become ten per cent and, again unlike the old system, the company doesn't have to pay the ten per cent over to HM Revenue & Customs (HMRC) and it's for this reason that the tax, not having been paid, is not refundable to the shareholder under any circumstances by the company paying the dividend. The ten per cent rate will continue to apply from 6 April 2008. Also, from 6 April 2008, the non-repayable ten per cent dividend tax credit will be extended to non-UK resident companies, provided that the investor owns less than ten per cent of the shares.

The effect of this is that the number and size of tax refunds taxpayers can claim each year has dropped dramatically.

The dividends to enter on your Tax Return each year are those paid in the tax year, regardless of when they were declared or the accounting year they related to.

How do I pay the tax on interest I receive that is not taxed at source?

Most interest is taxed at source and if at the end of the tax year too much tax has been deducted from a taxpayer's income, the tax suffered on interest payments can be refunded.

However, in some cases, interest is paid gross and under those circumstances the gross interest has to be reported on the Tax Return and any underpayment of tax worked out on the tax calculation sheets.

What is the tax position on bank interest?

Most bank interest is now paid net of tax. Taxpayers in receipt of interest from a bank should ask that bank to send them a certificate at the end of the tax year showing the gross interest, the tax deducted from it and the net figure. Those three figures will be entered on the Tax Return, either on their own or when added to other bank interest figures.

What is the tax position on building society interest?

Building society interest is very much like tax on bank interest (see above). Some building society interest is paid gross, in which case no tax repayment is possible; but if you have a building society account and have received net interest, at the end of the tax year you should ask them to send you a certificate of interest paid.

What is the tax position on annuities?

Annuities are sources of income usually enjoyed by the elderly. The taxpayer makes an investment in the annuity and over the remaining period of their life receives payments in connection with this annuity, some of which is capital and some of which is taxable income. When the annuity is paid it will be clearly shown how much is capital (and this is not taxable), how much is income and how much tax has been deducted.

You should total the income elements of each payment (gross, tax and net) and enter them on your Tax Return.

What are ISAs?

ISA stands for Individual Savings Account. They are free from Income and Capital Gains Tax. The maximum annual investment is £7,200 of which £3,600 may be in cash.

What are Venture Capital Trusts?

Venture Capital Trusts were introduced to encourage individuals to invest indirectly in unquoted trading companies. If you do this, you will be exempt from tax on dividends and capital gains arising from shares acquired of up to £200,000 a year. In addition, Income Tax relief of 30 per cent applies on up to £200,000 in any tax year, if you subscribe for new shares which you then hold for at least five years.

What are Enterprise Zone Investments?

Enterprise Zone Investments should not be confused with the Enterprise Investment Scheme. There may be an element of overlap, but the point of Enterprise Zones is that they tend to be areas of high unemployment that are given special tax breaks.

Enterprise Zones are of more interest to those who wish to set up businesses in them and professional advice should be sought.

What is the Enterprise Investment Scheme?

The Enterprise Investment Scheme (EIS) was introduced to encourage individuals to invest directly in unquoted trading companies. If you do this, you will be exempt from tax on capital gains (but not dividends) arising from shares acquired of up to £500,000 a year. In addition, Income Tax relief of 20 per cent applies on up to £500,000 in any tax year, if you subscribe for new shares which you then hold for at least three years.

It's also possible to defer Capital Gains Tax on any asset by reducing that gain by the EIS investment. The tax becomes payable when the EIS shares are sold.

What are REITs?

A REIT is a Real Estate Investment Trust and was introduced to encourage investment in the property sector. It enables investors to invest in the property market without buying a property and provides tax breaks for property companies by exempting income and gains from tax.

Income paid to investors will be net of basic rate tax. So, if you receive a payment of £80, the gross figure you should put on your Tax Return is £100 from which tax at 20 per cent has been deducted and, if you are a basic rate taxpayer, no further tax is due. If you are liable to tax at 40 per cent, you will have to pay the extra 20 per cent under self-assessment. These payments are known as PIDs (Property Income Distributions). Just to make things confusing, some REITs will also pay dividends which come with a ten per cent credit (see the first section of this chapter). The voucher that accompanies the payment should make it clear whether the payment is a PID or a dividend.

CHAPTER 9

Life assurance policies

What do I need to know about the taxation of life assurance?

The answer to this is probably 'not very much'. Life assurance used to enjoy a highly favoured tax status, but since 1984 this has been reduced. Some benefits remain and the overall concept is dealt with below.

There are three main types of life assurance. Firstly, there is term assurance, the sum of which is only paid if you die during the term of the policy; there is no savings element in this policy, but they tend to be cheap. Secondly, there is whole of life assurance, whereby the sum is payable on your death at any time and thirdly, there is an endowment policy, where the amount assured is payable on your death within the term of the policy or at the policy's end.

If you invest now in a life assurance policy (normally called 'single premium bonds'), you will pay no basic rate Income Tax when you draw the money out from it. However, you may be liable to the balance between higher rate tax 40 per cent and the basic rate tax 20 per cent if certain circumstances apply.

If what follows sounds complicated, don't worry, because the life assurance company is bound to send not only you, but also HM Revenue & Customs (HMRC), a certificate detailing the information about your policy and the gain that you have made.

In principle, if you withdraw no more than five per cent of your investment each year, there will be no further tax implications on this sort of policy. If you withdraw more than five per cent, there may be tax to pay, but we do suggest that rather than going into the complicated calculations in this book, you should take advice from either HMRC or a qualified accountant.

What are chargeable events?

A chargeable event is when you withdraw money from a life assurance policy or bond. As you will see from the previous question, unless you withdraw more than five per cent of your investment in any tax year, there will be no tax implications.

What are bonds?

There are all sorts of bonds, including Euro Bonds, Guaranteed Income Bonds and Single Premium Bonds. The subject of Euro Bonds doesn't really fall into the scope of this book, but in the case of Guaranteed Income Bonds these resemble annuities and only the income element is subject to Income Tax.

In the case of chargeable income bonds, we refer you to the question above relating to the taxation of life assurance, where we hope you will find the answer.

What is 'top slicing relief'?

Top slicing relief is complicated and we do suggest that, if you want a full answer which you will properly understand, you either attend the local Tax Office or refer to a professional adviser. Basically, it's a relief available to individuals (but not to companies) against what otherwise would be a higher rate of tax on any investment gain you might make on the surrender or sale of a life assurance policy.

What are 'partial surrenders'?

If you make a partial surrender of a life assurance policy, and this is usually the case when you receive annual payments from a single premium bond, it may give rise to tax but only if you withdraw more than five per cent of your original investment.

As with areas of this chapter on life assurance policies, we recommend you take professional advice, because the explanation of this complicated area of the tax law is beyond the ambit of this book.

Can I claim tax relief on my permanent health insurance payments?

Permanent health insurance policies are intended to provide you with an income should illness prevent you from working. If your employer pays the premium on your policy, they will obtain a tax allowance on the payment they make and you will have to pay tax on any benefit that you receive.

If you make the payments, whether as an employee or as a self-employed person, you won't obtain any tax relief, but any benefits paid to you under these circumstances would be tax free.

What are 'purchased life annuities'?

Purchased life annuities are investments normally taken out by the elderly which receive favourable tax treatment, but do contain substantial risk.

The basic principle is that you invest a lump sum with an insurance company; then each year, up until the day of your death, it will repay part of the capital together with interest. The interest is taxed but the capital is not. This is one way of increasing the spendable income of elderly people. However, the danger is that if an annuity is taken out on day one and the annuitant dies on day two, all the money is lost.

CHAPTER 10

Capital Gains Tax

What is Capital Gains Tax?

If you make a gain on the disposal of any investments, land and buildings, jewellery, antiques or any form of other property, you may be liable to Capital Gains Tax.

What does Capital Gains Tax catch and what does it not catch?

The main activities that we, as accountants, see our clients paying Capital Gains Tax on are as follows:

- Sale of businesses
- Sale of stocks and shares
- Sale of antiques over £6,000
- Sale of property
- Gifts of any of the above

Here is a list of some of the assets that are exempted from the Capital Gains Tax net:

- Private motor vehicles
- Your own home (but not including a second home)
- National Savings Certificates
- Foreign currency
- Decorations for gallantry (unless purchased)
- Betting winnings (including pools, lotteries and Premium Bonds)
- Compensation or damages for any wrong or injury suffered
- British Government Securities
- Life assurance policies and annuities
- Chattels (i.e. movable possessions) sold for £6,000 or less
- Assets given to a charity or the nation
- Enterprise Investment Scheme shares held for three years
- Timber and uncut trees
- Individual Savings Accounts
- Venture Capital Trust shares held for five years
- Guns, wine, antiques – providing they are not used in a business
- Debts
- Qualifying Corporate Bonds
- Child Trust Funds
- Cashbacks

A rough guide to Capital Gains Tax is provided at Appendix 7.

What are the new rules introduced on 6 April 2008?

For **individuals, partnerships and trusts**, from 6 April 2008 the rate of Capital Gains Tax is 18 per cent. This is charged on all gains above the annual exempt amount, which for 2008/09 is £9,600. The chargeable gain is the difference between the sale proceeds (less costs of sale) and original cost or market value at 31 March 1982 if later, plus any improvement costs incurred in the intervening period. There is no inflation allowance and no taper relief. Capital losses may be deducted from capital gains or, if these are insufficient, carried forward to subsequent years.

The chargeable gains of **companies** are included in their total taxable profits for the relevant period. They are calculated as for individuals with one exception: companies may claim an Indexation Allowance to take account of inflation. The Retail Prices Index – from March 1982 onwards – is applied to the period of ownership of the asset to calculate this.

What is entrepreneurs' relief?

A new relief is introduced to give preferential treatment for the disposal of business assets. This term includes trading businesses either carried on alone or in partnership, assets of that business, shares in the individual's own trading company and assets owned by the individual but used in their trading company or business. Furnished holiday letting properties are also regarded as business assets, but not properties used for any other type of letting. The relief reduces the amount of the gain chargeable to tax by 4/9ths, so that when the resulting gain is charged to tax at 18 per cent it's equivalent to ten per cent on the whole of the gain.

There is a lifetime limit of £1m upon which the entrepreneurs' relief can be claimed and claims can be made on more than one occasion to utilise the lifetime limit. The business must have been owned for at least one year ending on the date of the disposal.

Who pays Capital Gains Tax?

The quick answer is: the person making the gain; but where an asset is given away and the taxpayer may think that they have made no gain (because no money has been received) and therefore have no tax to pay, they may easily be mistaken. Because a gift constitutes a disposal, if there is a gain on that disposal, even the giver, who is in receipt of no disposal proceeds, pays Capital Gains Tax on the gain that they are deemed to have made on the disposal.

To pay Capital Gains Tax one has to be a UK resident taxpayer, which includes a company, trust or partnership.

However, if you are resident but not domiciled in this country, you are only charged Capital Gains Tax on your overseas realisations of assets when you bring the money here.

Is there an annual exemption from Capital Gains Tax?

Every year there is an annual exemption from Capital Gains Tax and in the year 2008/09 your first £9,600 of gains is exempt. In the case of trusts, it's £4,800.

The rate of Capital Gains Tax is 18 per cent for individuals, partnerships and trusts.

What can I set against my Capital Gains Tax liability?

Apart from the annual exemption, you are entitled to set the costs of acquisition of the asset, including purchase price, and the sale costs against the gain.

In addition, if you bought an asset on which you have incurred enhancement or improvement expenditure, then that too will be allowed as a cost. Certain costs such as accountant's fees are not allowed, but if you are looking for allowable costs, and because this subject can be so wide-ranging, we suggest you talk either to a professional accountant or to HM Revenue & Customs (HMRC).

Can I get any relief for capital losses?

If you sell or give away a capital asset at a loss, it's normally deductible from any capital gains that you have made during the same year and any remaining unrelieved losses are available to carry forward against future capital gains. If you give or sell an asset to a 'connected person' (generally a blood relative or a business partner/fellow director), the loss can only be used against gains on assets sold to the same party.

However, there is some relief available from a different quarter. If you make a trading loss in your business and don't have enough income to cover it, you can elect for the unused losses from that trading period to be set against your capital gains for that same tax year or for the previous tax year. In other words, capital gains can be reduced by trading losses. Again, we would suggest that you seek professional advice or help from the taxman on this.

How and when is Capital Gains Tax paid?

Capital Gains Tax is payable by individuals on 31 January following the end of the tax year in which the gain was made. It's payable by companies, along with the rest of their Corporation Tax, nine months after their year end.

What are the rules for part-disposals?

Where part of an asset is disposed of, you have to work out the cost applicable to the part sold.

The rules are complicated. A special rule applies to small part-disposals of land and, provided that the sale proceeds don't exceed either £20,000 or one fifth of the total market value of the land, you may deduct the sale proceeds from your base cost rather than pay any tax now.

What are the rules for private residences and Capital Gains Tax relief?

Normally, the house or flat in which you live is exempt from Capital Gains Tax when you sell it. The property must have been your only or main residence during the period of ownership. During the last 36 months of ownership, the property is always regarded as your main residence even if you don't live there. You can also be absent for periods totalling three years and for any period throughout which you worked abroad. To qualify for these additional periods of exemption, you must live in the property both before and after the absence. In addition, if you had any work which required you to live in job-related accommodation, that also doesn't stand against you for Capital Gains Tax purposes. Any periods of absence in excess of the periods allowed result in the relevant proportion of your sale profit being charged to Capital Gains Tax.

If a specific part of your house is set aside for business purposes, then that proportion of your profits on the sale of the house will be taxable. However, if you don't have any rooms used exclusively for business purposes you won't normally be liable to any Capital Gains Tax if you sell your house.

Special consideration needs to be given to houses with a lot of land alongside them. If land is sold in excess of what HMRC regards to be a normal area of garden in character for the house that is being sold, then the gain on the sale of such extra land will be subject to Capital Gains Tax.

If you owned two properties, within two years of buying the second one you should have sent in a letter (called an 'election') in which you disclosed to the taxman which you were treating as your private residence for Capital Gains Tax purposes. Otherwise, the taxman will decide for you and the decision will be based on the facts.

What are the rules for chattels sold for less than £6,000?

A chattel is an asset which is 'tangible movable property', such as a work of art or a set of chairs. Provided that the asset fetches no more than £6,000, HMRC doesn't require you to pay Capital Gains Tax on it. However, if you have a set of dining room chairs and while each one is not worth £6,000 but in total the set is worth say £30,000, the set will attract Capital Gains Tax on it, because a set is treated as one chattel.

What Capital Gains Tax relief is there for the disposal of business assets?

In principle, you are liable to Capital Gains Tax in respect of any assets used in your business. However, if all of the disposal proceeds are invested in further business assets that are purchased within one year before or three years after the sale, you can claim 'rollover relief' as a result of which the gain on the disposal is deducted from the cost of the new business assets acquired. Therefore, no tax is paid until the new business assets are sold, unless they too are replaced. For these assets to qualify they must either be land and buildings, fixed plant and machinery, goodwill, milk and potato quota or other agricultural quotas including payment entitlements under the Single Payment Scheme. Please note that motor vehicles or any vehicle on wheels don't qualify.

What Capital Gains Tax relief is there for gifts?

In principle, gifts of assets don't escape Capital Gains Tax, but gifts of the following attract a special relief called 'holdover relief':

- Business assets
- Agricultural property
- Shares and securities in a family trading company
- A gift which gives rise to an immediate charge to Inheritance Tax

Gifts which attract Inheritance Tax are rare, but one such example is when you transfer assets into a discretionary trust. Gifts to individuals and to trusts for disabled people, are classed as potentially exempt transfers (PETs) and Inheritance Tax won't be payable, unless you die within seven years of making the gift. However, tapering relief may reduce the Inheritance Tax payable after three years.

What are the aspects of Capital Gains Tax if I live abroad?

If you are resident and ordinarily resident in this country (see page 125 for further information on these terms), you are liable to tax on any capital gains realised anywhere in the world. However, if you have realised a gain in a country which won't allow the proceeds to be sent to the UK, you can claim for the gain to be deferred until the year in which you receive the money in this country.

If you are non-resident in this country but are carrying on a trade in the UK, you are liable to Capital Gains Tax on the assets used in the business. If you are UK domiciled, HMRC does have new powers to apportion certain capital gains of overseas trusts of which you are a beneficiary and this has caught out a number of wealthy people who transferred their assets abroad.

If you leave the UK for tax residence abroad you must be absent for at least five years if you wish your capital gains in the UK or abroad to be UK tax free. This is a complicated matter and professional advice should be sought. The table in Appendix 8 may help.

Can I sell shares one day, creating enough gains to use up the annual Capital Gains Tax allowance, and buy them back the next day?

Unfortunately, the Government stopped this loophole in 1998. If you sell shares and buy them back within 30 days (known as the 30-day rule), for Capital Gains Tax purposes the disposal of the shares is matched against the purchase cost of the shares acquired within 30 days of the sale, not against the original acquisition cost. However, you can get around this problem if your spouse buys the shares back on the open market, and not directly from you.

CHAPTER 11

Trusts and estates

What is a trust?

A trust is brought into existence when a person (called the 'settlor') transfers some of their assets to trustees (who become the legal owners) for the benefit of third parties, called 'beneficiaries' (the beneficial owners). A trust is a legal entity in itself. Another word for a trust is a settlement. Sometimes trusts are created under a Will and sometimes they are created during the lifetime of the settlor. Sometimes trusts are created to save tax, sometimes to protect assets; there are many and various reasons for setting up a trust.

Does a trust have to complete a Tax Return and what tax does a trust pay?

Trusts, or rather trustees, do have to complete a Tax Return reporting their income and capital gains on an annual basis, although this is often prepared by an accountant. In cases where the beneficiaries have a life interest in the income of the trust (known as interest in possession trusts), the appropriate lower rate of tax is paid by the trustees and the beneficiaries are treated as having paid the tax that has been deducted by the trustees.

In the case of discretionary trusts (and again we are verging into the area where professional advice should be sought) sufficient extra tax must be paid to bring the total tax up to 40 per cent, which is the rate for discretionary trusts.

The tax the trusts pay is paid on 31 January and 31 July each year.

How are trusts in Wills affected by tax?

The main tax that affects Wills, triggered by the death of the person, is Inheritance Tax and there is a separate section in this book dealing with this very aspect. However, when someone dies their personal representative (PR) or executor will make sure that a personal Tax Return is completed from the start of the tax year to the date of the deceased's death. From the date of their death to the end of the tax year the PR will have to account for tax and report to the beneficiaries on the tax that the PR has deducted. Each year the PR will have to submit an Income Tax Return to HM Revenue & Customs (HMRC). However, in the year in which the estate is wound up and all the assets have been distributed, the PR will only have to account for the tax on the income up to the date of distribution. In practice, if probate value is less than £2.5 million and the total tax due by the PR is less than £10,000, HMRC will accept a single computation and one-off payment.

What are accumulation and maintenance settlements (A&M trusts)?

An accumulation and maintenance settlement is a settlement normally created for the benefit of a minor where the income from a trust is accumulated and not distributed until the beneficiaries reach the age of at least 18. The income from such trusts is taxed at 40 per cent, with the exception of dividends, which are taxed at 32.5 per cent.

However, in his 2006 Budget the Chancellor introduced measures which, with effect from 6 April 2008, subject existing A&M trusts to broadly the same regime as discretionary trusts. These measures took effect on 22 March 2006 for new trusts and the addition of new assets to existing trusts.

We explain these new measures under the section 'Trust modernisation' on page 112.

What are discretionary trusts?

A discretionary trust is one in which the settlor gives discretion to the trustees as to how they treat the income and capital and to whom they distribute it. These trusts also pay Income Tax at the rate of 40 per cent (and 32.5 per cent on dividends).

How do discretionary trusts pay Inheritance Tax?

A discretionary trust doesn't pay Inheritance Tax on a death, but it does pay Inheritance Tax on every tenth anniversary of the date of settlement if this was after 31 March 1983. The charge, called 'the periodic charge', is at 30 per cent of the lifetime rate, which is itself half of the rate on death. In principle, the rate of tax is therefore six per cent (i.e. 30 per cent × 20 per cent) of the assets in the trust, but the calculation is not an easy one and you should seek professional advice.

A discretionary trust also pays Inheritance Tax when any of the settled property leaves the trust. This is called an 'exit charge'. The rate of tax is determined by the length of time that has elapsed either since the creation of the trust or since the last periodic charge.

How do trusts pay Capital Gains Tax?

Most trusts attract half the annual exemption that is available for individuals. This is currently half of £9,600, i.e. £4,800 (for 2008/09). The capital gains are worked out in accordance with the usual Capital Gains Tax rules (see chapter 10) and the tax on any capital gain is paid over at the same time as the balancing payment for the Income Tax, in other words 31 January following the end of the tax year. Trusts pay Capital Gains Tax at the rate of 18 per cent.

Trust modernisation

In 2003, the Chancellor announced plans to simplify and modernise the tax system for trusts. Initially, he began with these two:

1. From 6 April 2005 discretionary trusts and accumulation and maintenance trusts have a standard rate band of £1,000. What this means in practice is that the first £1,000 of income is charged at either ten per cent, 20 per cent or 22 per cent. Income in excess of £1,000 will be taxed at 32.5 per cent or 40 per cent.

2. From 6 April 2004 certain trusts with vulnerable beneficiaries are able to elect that the trust income and gains is taxed at the beneficiaries' tax rate if this proves more beneficial.

In his 2006 Budget, however, he created an uproar amongst trustees, beneficiaries and their professional advisers with the following series of measures against trusts.

1. From 22 March 2006 gifts to either accumulation and maintenance settlements or interest in possession settlements (whether new or existing trusts) are regarded as chargeable transfers for Inheritance Tax purposes. This means that transfers into them above the nil-rate band are subject to tax at 20 per cent.

   New trusts are subject to the ten-year charge of six per cent and, like discretionary trusts, there is also an exit charge from such trusts.

   These new charges do not apply to trusts for the disabled. Nor do they apply to a trust set up in a parent's Will for a minor child, so long as they are fully entitled to the assets at the age of 18.

   In other words, broadly speaking, the regime that used to apply to discretionary trusts now applies to these other types of trust as well.

2. From 6 April 2008, existing accumulation and maintenance trusts are also caught by these rules, unless they have revised their trust deed to allow the beneficiary to receive the funds by the age of 18.

3. It was generally felt by the accountancy and legal profession that making significant sums available at the age of 18 was unwise. As a result of representations, the Government only made one small

concession. A new type of trust has been created, known as an age 18 to 25 trust. With such trusts, the beneficiary doesn't have to take capital at the age of 18, but must do so by the age of 25. For these trusts, there is no exit or ten-year charge while the beneficiary is under the age of 18. From 18 to 25 a reduced Inheritance Tax charge applies. The maximum payable is 4.2 per cent (instead of six per cent). Some parents may feel that paying tax at 4.2 per cent maximum is a better option than handing over a large capital sum to an 18 year old.

4. From 22 March 2006, when an interest in possession trust comes to an end so that the property remains on trust, this is treated as the creation of new settled property. There is an immediate entry charge.

It has to be said, with the Government having said that it supported the use of trusts, this new regime flies in the face of such a declaration.

CHAPTER 12

Corporation Tax

What is Corporation Tax?

Corporation Tax is the tax that limited companies and unincorporated associations (such as clubs) pay on their profits. It's a tax on the profits of the company; profits include interest and capital gains.

How is Corporation Tax assessed and paid?

Corporation Tax is accounted for in 12-month periods, unless the accounting period from its commencement to the first accounting date, or the last period of operation, is less than 12 months. (You may already be thinking that it's time to consult a professional accountant and, in our view, if you have a limited company and you are dealing with Corporation Tax you should certainly seek professional advice.) Every company has to fill in an annual Corporation Tax Return (Form CT600) and this Return has to be submitted by the company secretary or the directors within 12 months of the end of the accounting period. However, tax has to be paid, assuming we are dealing with a small company, nine months after the end of the accounting period. Big companies have to pay Corporation Tax at more frequent intervals.

What is Corporation Tax Self-Assessment?

Corporation Tax Self-Assessment was introduced for all companies, clubs and unincorporated associations' financial years ending after 1 July 1999.

It was not a big change because already companies, etc. had to work out their tax and pay it without the aid of HM Revenue & Customs (HMRC).

What has changed is that Corporation Tax assessments are no longer being issued. The Corporation Tax Return is structured so that the tax liability can be worked out automatically. When HMRC sends you the notice to send it a Corporation Tax Return, there is a payslip attached to the bottom of the notice.

How are company profits calculated?

In principle, company profits are calculated in the same way as profits for non-incorporated businesses. However, this book doesn't pretend to be the only tool you need to calculate your company's profits properly.

What do I have to do about the Corporation Tax Return?

When the Corporation Tax Return arrives, we strongly suggest you send it to your accountant and get them to complete it for you. This will normally be done once the accounts have been prepared.

What is the rate of Corporation Tax and how does the small company rate of tax work?

There are two rates of Corporation Tax – the small companies rate and the full rate. The small companies rate is at 21 per cent on profits up to £300,000. Companies with profits over £1,500,000 pay the full rate of 28 per cent. Marginal relief operates in between and this has the interesting effect of taxing profits in the marginal bands more highly than profits above the upper limit!

The rates are summarised below:

Profits (£)	Tax rate
First 300,000	21%
300,001 to 1,500,000	29.75%
Over 1,500,000	28%

When is a company trading and how does this affect its tax position?

A company is trading once it has sold something. It's also trading if it has been incorporated and has begun to develop and manufacture goods or services. Any loss that it makes will be carried forward until it makes its first profit. The loss can then be used to reduce the first profits.

Do dormant companies have to pay Corporation Tax?

Dormant companies are, by definition, those that are doing nothing and, although a Corporation Tax Return may have to be submitted, there would be no tax to pay.

Under recent legislation it's possible for a dormant company to do certain minor things (such as issue shares and pay the annual return fee), but this doesn't constitute the earning of taxable profits.

What are 'associated' and 'subsidiary' companies?

Associated companies are those that are under common control or where one controls the other.

A subsidiary company is one that is either wholly or substantially owned by another company.

What is the significance of a 'close company'?

A close company is, broadly speaking, a company that is under the control of five or fewer 'participators'. A participator is a person having a share or interest in the capital or income of the company. It's defined broadly to include, for example, any loan creditor of the company and any person who possesses a right to receive or participate in distributions of the company. A quoted company is not a close company if more than 35 per cent of its voting shares are owned by the general public.

Close companies used to be subject to special provisions, but the only provision that applies now is where they make loans or distributions to their directors. When this happens tax has to be charged on the loan or distribution, unless the loan is repaid before the tax is due.

What is the difference between a public and a private company?

A public company is a company limited by shares or guarantee, having a share capital and:

- the Memorandum of Association of which states it to be a public company;

- that has been registered as such;

- whose name ends 'public limited company' or plc;

- which has an allotted share capital of not less than £50,000 of which at least 25 per cent has been paid on issue.

All other companies are private companies. A private company that incorporates some but not all of these features remains a private company.

Note: Although private companies have advantages over public companies, trading under any sort of incorporated structure attracts extra hassle and administration. Professional advice must be sought.

What do UK companies with overseas income have to do about it?

A company that has overseas income has to pay Corporation Tax on the gross amount of such income, but double tax relief is usually available. If a UK company receives a dividend from an overseas company from which tax has been deducted, as we have said, the gross dividend is included in the taxable profits. However, there are other rules and we do suggest that you refer to specialist advice for help.

What are the tax rules about companies buying their own shares?

In the case of a small company, it's frequently difficult for a buyer to be found for the shares of a shareholder who wishes to retire or sell up. There are now rules which enable companies to buy their own shares but, once again, we suggest that professional advice is sought on this. Briefly, the rules are that:

- the company must not be quoted and should be trading or be the holding company of a trading company;

- the purchase of the shares by the company must be mainly to benefit the trade of the company;

- the shareholder must be UK resident and must have owned the shares for at least five years. In addition, their shareholding must be substantially reduced and this usually means by at least 25 per cent;

- if the payment is used to pay Inheritance Tax, within two years after death the above provisions do not apply.

How do I pay myself from my company?

In principle, you can either pay yourself a salary (which could be in the form of a bonus or other remuneration) or, so long as you hold shares in the company and there are the profits out of which to pay it, you could be paid a dividend.

If you are paid a salary, normal PAYE rules apply. If you are paid a dividend, the company doesn't have to pay any tax over at the time of making the distribution. This is because dividends can only be paid out of profits which have already been taxed. In principle, dividends are a more tax-efficient way of withdrawing profits from a company than salary. If you have lent money to your company and that company wishes you to be able to withdraw some of that loan (to have it paid back), there would be no tax involved with any such repayment.

What are the tax rules about a company paying dividends?

If a company pays a dividend, since 6 April 1999 it no longer has to pay any tax (called 'Advance Corporation Tax') over to HMRC. In the old days, this tax used to be used to reduce the eventual Corporation Tax due. Under the new rules, with no Advance Corporation Tax being paid, the full sum of Corporation Tax has to be paid nine months after the end of the accounting year.

In the hands of the shareholder, the tax credit which is included on the dividend voucher is not available for a refund, but it does count for all the tax that has to be paid by basic rate taxpayers.

How does a company get relief for its losses?

This is a large subject but we will try to give the basic rules as simply as we can.

A trading loss made in an accounting period can be set off against any other income and gains of the same period. Any surplus can then be carried against the profits for the preceding year or it can be carried forward and set off against the profits of future years. A loss in the final period can be carried back for three years.

How does group relief for losses work?

The trading losses of members of a group of companies can be used to reduce the trading profits of other members of the group, provided that:

- a claim is made within two years of the end of the accounting period;

- the companies participating in the relief are all based in the UK and the parent has at least 75 per cent interest in each of the subsidiaries, directly or indirectly. A company may be based outside of the UK without jeopardising the existence of a group but it may not itself participate in the relief.

Please note that even though the parent may only own 75 per cent of the shares, it's entitled to 100 per cent of the relief. Also note that capital losses cannot be group relieved.

There are complicated rules where a company joins or leaves a group during an accounting period – this is another reason for seeking professional advice.

How does a company pay Capital Gains Tax?

Companies pay Corporation Tax on their capital gains. Companies can still claim indexation relief (unlike individuals, partnerships and trusts).

Trading losses in accounting periods may be set off against not only gains, but also trading profits of the same period or indeed the previous period. Capital losses incurred by a company can only be offset against capital gains of the company in the same period or future accounting periods.

The rollover relief described on page 107 is also available to companies. In addition, if one company in a group has a gain, another company in the group can purchase a qualifying business asset and roll the gain into the purchase, deferring any charge to Corporation Tax.

Similarly, if one company has unused capital losses and another group company is to make a disposal which results in a capital gain, the company with the losses can be deemed to be making the disposal so that its losses can be used against the gain.

The rules are complicated and professional advice must be sought.

Can a director borrow money from their company?

In principle, it's illegal for a director to borrow money from their own company. Small expense sums are allowed to be borrowed in advance. If the loan has not been repaid nine months after the end of the company's financial year, tax at the rate of 25 per cent has to be paid on the sum borrowed (this sum is repaid by HMRC when the loan is repaid). If no interest or a beneficial rate of interest is paid on the loan (unless the loan is for £5,000 or less), a benefit in kind arises on which the director must pay Income Tax and the company Class 1A National Insurance contributions. The short answer to this question is 'no'.

Do companies claim capital allowances, agricultural and industrial buildings allowances in the same way as sole traders and partnerships?

The normal capital allowances rules for businesses apply to companies, but there are special rules and we suggest that professional advice is sought.

At what level of profits should I incorporate my business?

It all depends, and there is no one size fits all. There are many factors to consider and tax is only one aspect. It was thought that legislation on 'income shifting' would be introduced in the 2008 Budget. This entails allocating income to the spouse paying tax at the basic rate instead of the higher-rate spouse taking it all. Needless to say, HMRC would like the higher-rate spouse to pay the tax, but have bowed down to pressure and have put this on hold for a year to allow for further consultation – so watch this space as there is likely to be something in the 2009 Budget.

What are Personal Service Companies and how are they taxed (IR35)?

The so-called IR35 rules prevent someone (a worker) who works predominantly for just one business (a client), trading as a limited company (the intermediary) and then paying themselves dividends from the profits, thus avoiding National Insurance altogether.

Before we outline the rules, here are some definitions:

A worker will be caught by the rules if they:

- trade as a limited company (the intermediary); and
- control more than five per cent of the dividends; and
- receive or could receive payments from the intermediary which under normal circumstances would be paid to them as salary.

Partnerships are also caught:

- if the worker, together with their close family, are entitled to more than 60 per cent of the profits of the partnership; or
- where most of the profits come from working for a single client; or
- where a partner's profit share is based on their income from relevant contracts.

Now for the rules:

In the circumstances where a worker provides their services to one client for a contract lasting for more than a month, the rules state the following:

- You take the amount of cash and non-cash benefits received by the intermediary.

- You then deduct any salary (actual salary) paid by the intermediary to the worker.

- You also deduct an allowable expense claim which is a flat rate allowance of a total of:

  - the business mileage allowances for travel to each engagement;

  - five per cent of the expenses paid by the intermediary for the contracts;

  - the expenses normally allowed to an employee;

  - the capital allowances normally allowed to an employee;

  - the employer's pension contributions;

  - the employer's National Insurance contributions.

- The balance (called 'deemed salary') is then treated as pay. Tax and National Insurance have to be applied accordingly.

- The tax and National Insurance arising on the balance are payable by 19 April after the year with interest running on late payments.

- Unpaid amounts can be recovered from the worker if the intermediary doesn't pay up.

There is one final twist; the deemed salary is not regarded as wages for the purpose of the National Minimum Wage, so the actual salary must be sufficient to meet the minimum wage requirements.

This is a nightmare, although it should be said that all other employees who are taxed under PAYE are following the proper rules, so why not these workers as well?

There are ways to escape from this net but space is not available here to explain what needs to be done. However, even if it's possible to escape, certain clients insist that their workers do trade as a limited company, to save themselves having to apply PAYE. Perhaps those who find that their clients insist on penalising them in this way should find other clients to work for?

CHAPTER 13

Non-residence, working overseas, etc.

What is the significance of my tax domicile?

Your domicile is the country which you regard as your natural home and the place where you intend to return in the event of going abroad. For most people it's the country of their birth and, unlike tax residence, it's not possible to have two domiciles under English law.

Up to 5 April 2008 foreign domiciled individuals who were UK resident paid UK tax on their UK income and capital gains and were entitled to claim UK personal allowances and the annual capital gains allowance. However, income and gains arising overseas only suffered UK tax if they were brought into the UK. From 6 April 2008 all this will change. The main change relates to non-domiciled individuals who have been UK resident for more than seven of the past ten years. If they wish to claim the remittance basis of assessment, they will have to pay an annual charge of £30,000 on top of the UK tax on their overseas income and gains. This won't apply if the unremitted income or gains is less than £2,000 and if this is the case, UK personal allowances and the annual capital gains allowance will also be available.

This is a complex area and anyone affected should seek specialist advice.

What is the significance of my tax residence?

Your tax residence is fixed by your circumstances of where you live and, when the figures and dates are worked out, how HM Revenue & Customs (HMRC) interprets your residence.

If you have always lived in this country, you are treated as being 'ordinarily resident' here.

If you have come to this country but intend to return to another, while HMRC will regard you as tax 'resident' it won't regard you as 'ordinarily resident' for tax purposes. Nowadays your residence position is not affected by you having a place of abode here provided that you are in full-time employment abroad. In other words, you may go abroad for a number of years to work and the fact that you still own a house in the UK doesn't mean that you are automatically considered to be a UK tax resident. If you wish to be considered as non-resident for tax purposes, you should spend a full tax year outside the country (although short periods in the UK may be disregarded by HMRC) and be able to show that you have left the UK in a meaningful way, rather than just being occasionally resident abroad.

What income is taxable and where?

If you are resident in this country, all normal taxable income, whether arising here or overseas, is taxable. However, if you are non-resident and you receive income from self-employment, partnerships or employment, all of which are carried out abroad, it will be tax free.

The rules are complicated so any aspect that needs further consideration should be referred for professional advice.

What is 'double taxation relief'?

The UK Government has entered into agreements with certain overseas countries (about 100 in all), the purpose of which is to prevent income and capital gains being taxed in both countries. So where income or capital gains have already been taxed in another country, in principle the foreign tax counts towards your UK tax bill. However, such overseas tax is not refundable.

How do I change my tax residence?

In order to change your tax residence, you can simply establish a permanent residence abroad and remain out of the country for a complete tax year (although in certain circumstances short visits are allowed). After that, you must avoid returning to the country for as much as six months in any one tax year and this must average at less than three months in the UK in every year.

When does someone who goes abroad become non-UK tax resident?

In principle, someone going to work full time abroad under a contract of employment will be treated as non-resident from the date they leave the UK. They must stay overseas for at least a full tax year. Visits to the UK are allowed but must be less than 183 days in any one year or 91 days on average over a four-year period. If you go abroad for any other reason, HMRC may give a temporary non-residence ruling and then review the position fully after three full years.

What tax do I pay on foreign income?

If you are a UK resident you pay normal UK tax on income from abroad, but if any of that foreign income has already suffered Income Tax in the country of origin, then it's more than likely that double taxation relief will result in that tax going towards paying your UK tax bill. However, the foreign tax cannot be refunded.

What tax do I pay on foreign pensions?

For people who are resident, ordinarily resident and domiciled in the UK, there is a ten per cent deduction permitted from their foreign pension before calculating the tax liability which arises from it.

If the foreign pension is paid as a result of Nazi persecution, then no liability to UK tax arises.

What is the tax position on professions conducted partly abroad?

If you work in any profession that is conducted partly within this country and partly overseas, you will normally be assessed to UK tax on your entire profits and it's only if you conduct a separate profession entirely abroad that special rules will apply.

What tax do I pay on earnings from overseas employment?

Again this is a tricky area, but, broadly, if you go to work abroad, so long as your absence lasts a whole tax year and your visits to the UK total less than 183 days in any tax year and on average are less than 91 days per year, you won't pay UK tax on your overseas earnings, and that includes your overseas earnings in the part of the tax year at the beginning of which you leave the UK and the part at the end of which you return.

What allowances can non-UK tax residents claim?

You may be able to claim UK tax allowances if you are not resident here. If you are eligible to claim you will generally be given the same allowances (i.e. the personal allowance) as an individual resident here. The following can claim, as well as certain others:

- A resident of the Isle of Man or the Channel Isles

- A citizen of the Commonwealth

- A citizen of a state within the European Economic Area

- A present or former employee of the British Crown

If I go abroad, do I have to pay tax on the rent I receive from letting out my home while I am away?

You will be liable to UK tax on the net rental income (i.e. gross rents less allowable expenses). Strictly speaking, the letting agent, or the tenant if there is no letting agent, should deduct tax at basic rate before paying the rent to you. However, you can apply to HMRC for a certificate authorising rental payments to be paid without deduction of tax.

You will still be entitled to your personal allowance and it may be that some of the tax that is deducted can be refunded to you. We strongly suggest you employ the services of an accountant to look after this for you.

Can I go abroad to avoid Capital Gains Tax?

This is a complicated matter and professional advice should be sought, but if you leave the UK for tax residence abroad, you should complete five tax years before you can be pretty confident that any capital gains, whether arising in the UK or abroad, won't be subject to Capital Gains Tax.

What should I do if I have just arrived in the UK to take up work here and will the rest of my overseas income be taxed?

In principle, you should contact the authorities or your employer will do this for you and from that day, even if it's the last day of the tax year, you will be entitled to the normal personal allowances. Equally, from that day you will be subject to Income Tax and National Insurance because you will be treated as a UK tax resident.

If you are self-employed or have income arising from a partnership or self-employment abroad or indeed interest arising abroad, then if you are UK resident but not UK domiciled, you will pay tax on income brought to the UK. If you are UK resident and UK domiciled, you will pay UK tax and may be able to claim double tax relief.

If I have just arrived in the UK, will the rest of my overseas income be taxed?

It depends on your residence and domicile status. See the final paragraph in the section above.

Should I put my money in an offshore trust?

The short answer is 'no'. In 1998, provisions were introduced whereby the UK tax, payable by beneficiaries of trusts who are not UK-resident, increased dramatically.

Foreign income and residence issues are summed up in the table at Appendix 8.

CHAPTER 14

Inheritance Tax

Note: From 6 December 2005 all references to married couples include same-sex couples who have registered as civil partners.

What is Inheritance Tax?

Inheritance Tax is basically the old 'death duties'. At one stage, some years ago, it was also called 'Capital Transfer Tax'. However, Inheritance Tax was introduced in the 1986 Finance Act and, although it's a highly complicated tax, certain basic information should be included in this book.

Inheritance Tax covers transfers on death and also chargeable lifetime transfers, such as transfers to discretionary trusts (unless they are set up for a disabled person). Chargeable lifetime transfers over the nil-rate threshold of £312,000 (2008/09) are taxed at the lifetime rate of 20 per cent. They may also be charged again on death if this occurs within seven years of the transfer but credit will be given for any lifetime tax paid.

Transfers to individuals and non-discretionary trusts are called 'potentially exempt transfers'. No Inheritance Tax is payable on these unless they occur within seven years of the transferor's death.

It's well worth bearing in mind that, starting at 40 per cent, Inheritance Tax is reaping far more for the Treasury than it used to and so this is a tax which should be attended to and, where possible, planning to minimise it should be put in place.

How and when is Inheritance Tax paid?

Inheritance Tax is due six months from the end of the month of someone's death. However, if a transfer is made which attracts Inheritance Tax during life, and that transfer is made between 6 April and 30 September, the due date for payment is 30 April in the following year. If the chargeable transfer is made between 1 October and 5 April, the due date is six months after the end of the month in which the transfer is made.

How should I approach the subject of Inheritance Tax?

As practising accountants, we hardly ever deal with Inheritance Tax matters ourselves, but we have been able to observe the way in which it's dealt with by other professional advisers and we have some fairly strong views on the subject.

Our view is that if you are worried about Inheritance Tax, on the whole, you should not go to a solicitor for advice but rather to a specialist Inheritance Tax adviser. While we don't like commenting on other professionals, we think that the following analysis is fair and appropriate. On the whole, chartered accountants are extremely competent at Income Tax, Capital Gains Tax, Value Added Tax as well as other accounting functions, but on the whole we should not advise our clients on matters of law. When it comes to solicitors, while they are very competent at matters of law, in our opinion only those who have the appropriate training and experience should advise their clients on matters of tax and particularly Inheritance Tax, where we have seen a number of bad mistakes made by people who have not been properly trained, who 'didn't know what they were doing'. So our advice is that Inheritance Tax planning should be dealt with by a specialist in Inheritance Tax matters. This is how we run our practice and how we advise our clients whenever they need Inheritance Tax advice.

Should I make a Will?

We always ask our clients if they have made a Will and try to make sure that, if they haven't, they do so quickly. If you haven't made a Will the chances are that, when you die, your assets won't go to the people you would like them to go to. It's not expensive drawing up a Will and we would strongly suggest you go to a solicitor to do so. However, in view of our comments about Inheritance Tax planning, we think it would be a good idea for you to ensure, before you visit the solicitor, that you have listed your assets, applied a rough valuation to them and seen if the Inheritance Tax bill for your estate is one that you are prepared to pay. If you are frightened by the size of the Inheritance Tax bill, then we suggest that you go to an Inheritance Tax specialist. Then, when you go to your solicitor, you can be armed with not only what you want to happen but how you want the Inheritance Tax matters to be dealt with. If you don't do it this way round, you may find that you have a solicitor who thinks they know about Inheritance Tax making all the plans for you and in our experience this can often end in problems, and major problems. However, you do need to make a Will.

A template to help you work out your Inheritance Tax bill and plan to make a Will is provided at Appendix 9.

How do I choose my executors?

In our view, it's extremely important to appoint executors whom your survivors like. We have seen cases where the executors who have been appointed were not liked by the surviving spouse and the misery caused by the death of the testator was exacerbated by the insensitivity of the executors. Therefore, don't choose your own friends just because you like them. Make sure your spouse likes them too and is happy for them to be appointed.

The new nil-rate band rules

The new Chancellor, Alistair Darling, in his first Pre-Budget Report announced that from 9 October 2007 married couples or civil registered partners will inherit each other's unused element of the nil-rate band on first death. So, each couple will have a joint nil-rate band of £600,000. This will increase to £700,000 in 2010–2011. If the couple's joint estate falls within the joint nil-rate band, they no longer have to worry about Inheritance Tax. Although this was possible to achieve before 9 October 2007, it involved setting up complicated Wills and trusts.

For everyone else, including unmarried couples, siblings living together and carers who have lived in and inherited the family home, the nil-rate band is £300,000, rising to £350,000 in 2010–2011.

How can I reduce Inheritance Tax?

This is such a big subject and the sums involved are so potentially enormous that we would not presume to give anything more than general advice in a book of this nature. However, there are certain general rules which we believe to be sound:

1. Review your existing Wills in the light of changes announced in the Pre-Budget Report of October 2007.

2. Don't give everything away before you die; if you do and you keep on living, what will you live on?

3. Consider taking advice from an Inheritance Tax specialist (as we keep on saying).

4. Keep your Will up to date.

5. Let your survivors know in advance if their lives are likely to be radically affected by your death. For instance, if you are a wealthy person and you wish to leave your money to somebody you don't see very often, it's not a bad idea to let that person know so that, in return for the anticipated inheritance, they look after you in your old age and are nice to you, etc. It's equally important to let those people know if you change your mind! There is this problem that Wills generate great anticipation and anxiety and it's as well not to be too secretive about what you are proposing to do, so as to reduce extra stress and burdens on your survivors after you have died.

What are periodic charges?

Discretionary trusts are subject to a charge to Inheritance Tax every ten years. In most cases, the nil-rate band (up to £312,000 for 2008/09) is taxed at nought per cent. Excess value over this is charged at 30 per cent of the lifetime rate of 20 per cent, i.e. six per cent.

What is 'quick succession relief'?

If, after someone dies and Inheritance Tax is paid on their estate, a beneficiary dies within five years, quick succession relief applies and the tax payable on the second death is at a reduced rate.

How will assets be valued?

In principle, on death your assets are valued for Inheritance Tax purposes at what they might reasonably be expected to fetch on the open market.

Help, I've done nothing about Inheritance Tax. What are the first few essential golden rules that I should follow?

1. **Make a Will.**

   If you don't make a Will, chances are that your assets on your death won't be distributed according to your wishes. However, before you make a Will, it would be a good idea to attend to item 2 so that when you visit your solicitor you can 'hit the ground running' and, at the outset, tell them what you want your Will to say.

2. **List your assets and decide to whom you would like them to pass.**

   Why not use the sheet in Appendix 9?

3. **Calculate the Inheritance Tax due.**

   Again, use Appendix 9 for this purpose.

4. **Decide how seriously you view the impact of any Inheritance Tax payable.**

   If you can tolerate the impact that Inheritance Tax may make on both your estate and your successors, then, so long as you have made a Will, you can probably rest at ease. However, having said 'probably', do remember that Inheritance Tax at 40 per cent can make a serious dent in your estate and, assuming you are not a tax expert, you might possibly overlook something and the situation may not be as lenient as you suppose. Accordingly, you may be well advised to take professional advice and get your Inheritance Tax calculation checked. As we say elsewhere in this chapter, the best professional advice on Inheritance Tax mitigation is to be gained from someone who specialises in Inheritance Tax mitigation and not necessarily from a high street accountant, financial adviser or solicitor. Therefore, choose your Inheritance Tax adviser very carefully.

5. **If you have an Inheritance Tax problem, then consult a suitably qualified adviser on how to mitigate the charge.**

   Then, having received such expert wisdom, set about putting their recommendations in place.

6. **If you want to take some elementary steps to reduce the impact of Inheritance Tax, and if you do nothing else, please at least consider the following possible courses of action:**

   - If you are currently unmarried or not in a civil registered partnership and you are facing an Inheritance Tax bill on your death, then we strongly suggest you follow steps 1 to 4 above.

   - If you survive your spouse or civil partner, make sure that you remember to utilise their unused nil-rate band.

   - Until the 2004 Budget changes, it was possible to pass your house into a trust which divides the freehold from a new leasehold. This new leasehold is something that you set up which is due to start a short time after your death. The existence of this leasehold drastically reduces the value of the freehold which you effectively give to your children when you set the trust up. So once you have lived for seven years after giving the house away, the house no longer forms part of your estate. If you die within seven years, the value of the house in your estate falls dramatically, because it's subject to a lease. However, from now on, if you do effect such a transfer of your home, you may have to pay rent to live in it, under the pre-owned assets rules, which we cover in chapter 2.

- Married couples and civil registered partners should review how to own their own home.

- When it comes to passing investments to your children, there are a number of excellent financial products (such as loan trusts and discounted gift schemes) which we have seen used to very good effect. One of the beauties of these schemes is that, while ensuring that the capital passes to the next generation in a tax efficient way, they can also (and usually do) increase your annual spending money.

- If you can afford to do so, use the nil-rate band to good effect. If you were to give away 1/7th of the nil-rate band every year (£44,500), by the time year seven had arrived, and assuming you are still alive, you would have given away at least £312,000 tax free. In year eight, the first gift would drop out of the equation, in year nine, the second and so on. If both you and your spouse do this, then you can give away £89,000 per year. However, do take professional advice.

- If you invest in shares in unquoted trading companies (including shares listed on the Alternative Investment Market), once you have owned them for two years, they should qualify for 100 per cent Inheritance Tax relief. However, be careful as the value of unquoted shares can just as easily go down as up.

- As part of your Inheritance Tax planning, try to ensure that you will have enough to live on!

What is a Gift with Reservation of Benefit?

If you give an asset away but continue to enjoy a benefit from it, you are said to have reserved a benefit and have not effectively given the asset away. It will therefore still form part of your estate on death.

In the case of giving a house away but still living in it, this won't be a gift with reservation if you pay the full market rent on the house.

As we have explained elsewhere, there is an Income Tax charge on pre-owned assets. The giver has to pay tax on the annual value of the benefit they have retained.

CHAPTER 15

VAT

What is VAT?

Value Added Tax is a tax imposed when goods or services are sold. Any business which has a turnover in excess of £67,000 should, in principle, register for VAT and add VAT to its VAT-able supplies.

This is a complicated subject and anyone running a business with a turnover approaching £67,000 should seriously consider approaching an accountant and consider whether they should register for Value Added Tax with HM Revenue & Customs (HMRC).

In the case of businesses with a turnover in excess of £67,000, they certainly should take professional advice because they may be starting to get into deep trouble.

What records do I need to keep if my business is VAT-registered?

We strongly suggest that you keep records, either on a computer or in a cash analysis book; all your VAT records should be kept for six years.

In addition to this, you need to keep your invoices on which you have claimed back VAT input tax. You also need to keep copies of your sales invoices on which you have recorded your output tax.

You have to remember that it's likely that you will be investigated by HMRC's officials more than once during the average life of a business. When they come to see you, they will be wanting to check that your accounts are in order and that your VAT Returns have been properly prepared. You should arrange your affairs in such a way that anyone can find their way from your original transactions through to the submissions to HMRC without too much difficulty. The technical term for this is an audit trail and we would strongly suggest that you ask a professional accountant for help in making sure that your records are complete and well-filed.

How do I complete my VAT Return?

For most VAT-registered traders, HMRC needs just four figures for the VAT Return:

1. **Output VAT** (box 1). This is the total of the VAT you have charged on your sales invoices during the period. If you complete the VAT Return under the cash accounting rules (if your turnover is less than £1,350,000), then your output tax is calculated on the cash received during the period and not on the invoices issued. The figure must include any VAT scale charge for private motoring (see below).

2. **Input VAT** (box 4). This is the VAT that you yourself have been charged on your purchases, etc. during the period. If you are registered for VAT, then nearly all the VAT you have been charged can be included in this box. If you complete the VAT Return under the cash accounting rules, then your input tax is calculated on the cash paid during the period and not on the invoices received. You may not reclaim VAT on business entertaining, goods or services used privately or on the purchase of motor cars. If you lease a car which has any element of private use, you can only reclaim half the input VAT. If you reclaim VAT on fuel, you must add the scale charge for your vehicle to the output VAT in box 1 (see below). In addition, if you make exempt supplies (a complicated area and one we don't propose dealing with in this book), you will be subject to different rules.

3. **Total outputs** (box 6). This is the sum of the invoices you have issued to your customers (the sales of standard and zero-rated goods and

services) during the period. This sum should exclude the VAT element. However, if you are cash accounting, you total the sum received from your customers during the period but exclude the VAT element.

4. **Total inputs** (box 7). This is the sum of the invoices you have received from your suppliers during the period. This sum should exclude the VAT element. However, if you are cash accounting, you total the payments you have made for standard and zero-related purchases during the period, less the VAT element. You should not include any exempt purchases, nor any drawings.

You will notice that there are five other boxes on the VAT Return:

- Boxes 2, 8 and 9 affect few small traders; if they affect you, you should seek professional advice.

- The only other boxes that affect everyone are boxes 3 (the total of boxes 1 and 2) and 5 (the sum of box 3 less box 4 if there is net VAT to be paid to HMRC and the sum of box 4 less box 3 if there is net VAT to be reclaimed by you).

Lastly, remember that you must send back the completed Return, together with a cheque for any payment of VAT, before the end of the following month.

What is the Fuel Scale Charge?

If you reclaim VAT on all your fuel including that used privately, you are deemed to be making a supply to yourself of the private fuel. This supply must have output tax on it, just like any other standard rated supply. HMRC has prescribed values for this supply, depending on the size of your engine and the type of fuel used. The rates are shown in Appendix 1. It follows that, if the scale charge exceeds the value of the input tax you actually suffer on fuel purchases, you are better off not claiming input tax at all on your fuel.

What is Annual Accounting for VAT?

If your turnover is less than £1,350,000, you may apply to HMRC not to fill in quarterly VAT Returns but, instead, to:

- pay a sum to it by direct debit each month;
- fill in a VAT Return once a year; and
- settle up any over or underpayment with it at the end of the year.

Once your turnover reaches £1,600,000 you are no longer eligible to be part of the scheme.

What is Cash Accounting for VAT?

If your turnover is less than £1,350,000, you may apply to HMRC to pay VAT to it only when your customers have paid you and not on the basis of the invoices you have raised, whether they have been paid or not. Equally, you may only claim input VAT once your purchase invoices have been paid.

Once your turnover reaches £1,600,000, you are no longer eligible to be part of the scheme.

What is the optional flat rate VAT scheme for small traders and is it worth joining?

This scheme is for businesses with a total turnover of less than £187,500 (including VAT) and turnover of less than £150,000 (excluding VAT).

Those who join the scheme won't need to keep a record of VAT input tax. You simply charge VAT to your customers as at present and record the VAT inclusive total charged to customers. You don't need to keep any record of the input tax incurred on your purchases. You then look up on the list of flat rate percentages, the rate applicable to your category of business and pay that percentage to HMRC.

Whether it would be worth your while joining the scheme will depend on your circumstances. To work out how you would be affected were you to join, you take your turnover for the last twelve months, add VAT and then apply the relevant percentage. If that is less than the total payments you have made to HMRC in the period, then you may be better off joining the scheme.

You will no longer be able to reclaim input VAT on your expenditure. There is an exception to this for capital expenditure on which input VAT may be reclaimed in the normal way.

However, there are planning opportunities available for traders who carry on more than one type of business and each would have a different flat rate percentage. The percentage to be used is that which would apply to the business whose activity accounts for the majority of the trade. Where the majority trade has a lower flat rate percentage than the secondary trade, there may be savings to be made.

If you want to join, you should telephone your local VAT office for an application form.

Table of flat rate percentages by trade sector

Trade sector (from 1 January 2004)	Flat rate percentage
• Retailing food, confectionery, tobacco, newspapers or children's clothing • Post offices	2
• Membership organisation • Pubs • Wholesaling food	5.5
• Farming or agriculture that is not listed elsewhere • Retailing that is not listed elsewhere • Wholesaling agricultural products	6
• Retailing pharmaceuticals, medical goods, cosmetics or toiletries • Retailing vehicles or fuel • Sport or recreation • Wholesaling that is not listed elsewhere	7

- Agricultural services   7.5
- Library, archive, museum or other
  cultural activity
- Manufacturing food
- Printing
- Repairing vehicles

- General building or construction   8.5
  services*
- Hiring or renting goods
- Manufacturing that is not listed elsewhere
- Manufacture yarn, textiles or clothing
- Packaging
- Repairing personal or household goods
- Social work

- Forestry or fishing   9
- Mining or quarrying
- Transport or storage, including
  freight, removals and taxis
- Couriers
- Travel agency

- Advertising   9.5
- Dealing in waste or scrap
- Hotels or accommodation
- Photography
- Publishing
- Veterinary medicine

- Any other activity not listed elsewhere   10
- Investigation or security
- Manufacturing fabricated metal products

- Boarding or care of animals   10.5
- Film, radio, television or video production

- Business services that are not listed   11
  elsewhere
- Computer repair services
- Entertainment or journalism
- Estate agency or property management
  services

- Laundry or dry-cleaning services
- Secretarial services

• Financial services	11.5
• Catering services, including restaurants and takeaways • Hairdressing or other beauty treatment services • Real estate activity not listed elsewhere	12
• Architect, civil and structural engineer or surveyor • Management consultancy	12.5
• Accountancy or book-keeping • Computer and IT consultancy or data processing • Lawyers or legal services	13
• Labour-only building or construction services*	13.5

* **Building or construction services**, use 'labour-only' if the value of materials supplied is less than ten per cent of your turnover. If the value of materials is more than this, builders use the 'general building' flat rate.

When can I deregister?

If your turnover is not going to exceed £65,000 in the coming 12 months, you can apply for deregistration.

CHAPTER 16

Stamp Duty

What is Stamp Duty?

Stamp Duty is payable on transfers of shares and certain other documents and it's quite complicated trying to work out whether something attracts Stamp Duty or not.

When it comes to share transfers, the amount of stamp duty payable is 50p for every £100 and is rounded up to the nearest £5. Stamp Duty is not payable on the issue of shares.

From 13 March 2008 transfers that would previously have attracted Stamp Duty of no more than £5 are now exempt.

It might be helpful to include a list of the instruments which require stamping:

- Stock and share transfers

- Declarations of trust

- Certain proxy forms

- Tenancy agreements where the gross rent is more than £5,000 per annum and is for a six- or twelve-month term

Certain Stock Transfer Forms only attract a fixed duty of £5, no matter what the transaction and these are listed on the Stock Transfer Form.

Transfers to, from or between trustees, transfers in connection with divorce, and transfers which are gifts don't attract Stamp Duty.

When and how is Stamp Duty paid?

Stamp Duty is assessed and paid by the person who is responsible for ensuring that it's paid. They send the document to the Stamp Duty Office (your local Tax Office will tell you where this is) to be stamped and the document will be returned to you stamped with the amount that you have paid.

If you happen to be in London, it's well worth a visit to Bush House in The Strand to see the Stamp Duty Office because in there you will see stamping machines which were made 70 years ago, still going strong. Maybe one day stamping will become electronic in one form or another, but at the moment it's performed by what can only be described as 'Green Goddesses'.

What is Stamp Duty Land Tax?

Stamp Duty Land Tax was introduced on 1 December 2003 and replaces the 'old' Stamp Duty on land.

In the case of freehold property, the Stamp Duty Land Tax payable by the purchaser is as follows:

	Non- residential and residential in disadvantaged areas £	Residential outside disadvantaged areas £
Zero	0–150,000	0–125,000
1%	150,001–250,000	125,001–250,000
3%	250,001–500,000	250,001–500,000
4%	Over 500,000	Over 500,000

Its introduction bites harder on leases than the old Stamp Duty but the rules and complicated calculations are outside the scope of this book. If you want to find out the details, we suggest you get hold of HM Revenue

& Customs' leaflet *A Guide to Leases*, which is Leaflet SD3 forming part of its Stamp Duty Land Tax range of publications.

It's now effectively a self-assessment tax, although the real practical significance is more for solicitors than anyone else, who have to ensure that their clients pay the right amount of tax.

CHAPTER 17

Other tax issues

Tax planning do's

- Buy your own house as soon as you can. Historically, houses have been a good investment. Any capital gain on your private residence will be tax free. However, by the same token there are no tax allowances for any losses on sale.

- Make sure you have got good pension and life assurance cover and keep the situation constantly under review.

- Make use (if you can afford to) of the £3,000 tax-free annual capital transfer (i.e. give this sum away Inheritance-Tax-free each year) and, if you did not use up last year's allowance, you can give away an additional £3,000.

- Always claim your personal and other tax allowances. This should normally be dealt with for you by HM Revenue & Customs (HMRC) but you should keep the matter under annual review (e.g. have you passed retirement age?).

- Claim all business expenses you are entitled to against any business profits – always keep a chit for petty cash expenses. If you don't, how will your accountant know you have incurred that particular expense?

- Pay your spouse properly for any work they do in your business. In the 2008/09 tax year, remember, they can earn £6,035 tax free, although payments over this sum will involve them paying National Insurance contributions.

- Consult with your stockbroker in order to make sure you take advantage of the annual £9,600 Capital Gains Tax relief, i.e. if you can make a gain of this size it will be tax free.

- Make a Will. You can create one inexpensively using Lawpack's *Last Will & Testament Kit* or you can take legal advice.

- Think carefully about providing funds to pay any Inheritance Tax on death (term assurance isn't very expensive).

- Plan ahead and, wherever possible, let your accountant know of your plans/ wishes so that you can be advised on any tax implications.

- Divide your assets and the related income with your spouse so that the best use is made of Income Tax lower and basic rate bands.

- Let an independent financial adviser give you the equivalent of a financial 'medical examination'.

- Ask your accountant to give a rough idea of your tax liability in January and July each year. Then divide the sum by 12 and start saving up for it by transferring the monthly figure to a deposit account. This way paying tax is much less painful.

Tax planning don'ts

There is a lot of what one might call 'pub chat' about tax – particularly on the subject of avoiding tax – and quite often the apparent expert is not giving the full picture. This is our attempt to give the tax novice some basic tax information so that they can tell whether the information coming across the crowded smoke-free room (or wherever) is accurate.

1. Don't avoid receiving income because it will have to have tax paid on it. If you earn £1 and pay the taxman 20p, you are still left with 80p and that is 80p more than you started out with. Whether you are prepared to do the work or whatever for a net benefit of 80p is another matter. The main argument, often put forward, that you won't be able to afford to pay the tax on any extra income is a false

one. If you receive income and pay tax on it, you are left with something. If you don't receive the income in the first place, you will be left with nothing.

2. Don't put tax saving first. Always put sound commercial or family considerations first and then fit the tax implications into what you want to do. If you own a business which is making money and paying tax, the key fact is that your business is making money. If your business is losing money and paying no tax, then the thing to concentrate on is not how marvellous it is that you are not paying tax but how vital it is to turn the business around and start making money. In the same way, but on a personal level, don't emigrate to a tax haven in order to save tax. Emigrate to a tax haven if you wish but your reason for doing so must not be to save tax but instead because you would rather live there than in the UK. If you don't like the place, why go to live there? Thus plan to do what you want to do first and then fit the tax implications into the picture.

3. Don't enter into tax-saving schemes, on the advice of either an accountant or anyone else, that run a long time. The law can change, your circumstances can change and either could make a nonsense of a long-term plan.

4. Don't automatically trust trusts. Be very careful about putting your money into trusts – particularly since 22 March 2006 (see chapter 11).

5. Don't give all your money away in order to save Inheritance Tax. If you do, what will you live on?

6. Don't make your affairs too complicated. Keep your affairs simple and flexible so that you can (a) understand what is going on and (b) make any changes as and when you want.

7. Don't try to cheat the taxman. Be honest in all your dealings. Keep proper records of all your transactions, especially cash receipts, and declare everything properly. If you don't, you will be found out.

Tax-saving tips

For employers, employees and company directors

- Shares: companies can offer shares to staff through a share option or share incentive scheme. The rules are complicated, but the chances of acquiring wealth in a tax-efficient way are very real. Talk to an accountant first.

- Company car: this is becoming less popular as the taxable benefit of having a car has increased so much in recent years that it's often better to give back the car and have extra salary instead. However, if you are prepared to drive a smaller highly fuel-efficient car, it may still be beneficial to have a company car.

- Company fuel: this is now so heavily taxed that it will rarely be beneficial for a company to provide fuel to its employees. You should ensure that there is an agreement in writing which requires you to reimburse your company for any private fuel used. Better still, buy your own fuel and reclaim from the company that which is used for business.

- Cheap loans to employees: in many cases, no taxable benefit arises in the case of a loan of up to £5,000.

- In general, all benefits are taxable, but meals provided free of charge (or at low cost) in a canteen on the firm's premises are not taxable if they are available to staff generally.

- HMRC's practice is not to tax expenditure of up to £150 per head on the annual Christmas party or a similar function (as long as it's open to all staff).

- Accommodation: a company may purchase a house for an employee to live in rent free. There may be a small amount of tax due on the value of the accommodation, etc., but the charge will be small in proportion to the benefits provided.

- Payments to private health care schemes, such as BUPA and PPP, are not taxable for lower-paid employees (defined as those receiving under £8,500 per annum, including the payments).

- Tax is not payable on financial rewards to staff for suggestions they may make on the running of a business. However, such 'suggestions schemes' must meet certain requirements.

- Incentive awards: employees can be given non-cash awards for meeting certain targets and, in addition, any tax that these might attract can be paid by the employer on the employees' behalf.

- Pension schemes: Employers can consider making pension schemes non-contributory. This way they can reduce payments they make to staff by the amount of the pension contributions the staff members have been making (in other words, the member of staff would be no worse off as a result of this) but the company would have less National Insurance contributions to pay on the lower salary figure.

- Company directors will be able to save themselves a little tax in the form of National Insurance contributions for themselves, if instead of receiving their pay in the form of salary they were to receive the equivalent sum in the form of rent for the company's use of property owned by the director, dividends on shares or interest from the loan made by the director to the company. However, you should seek professional advice.

- Loans to directors: it's illegal under company law for a company to lend any director money and, even if it's done, there are heavy tax penalties attached to this. Do consider the following points:

  1. Immediately before incorporation the business can take out a bank loan enabling you to withdraw a substantial sum in advance.

  2. You can arrange the capital structure of the company so that at least part of your investment is by way of a loan account against which you may be free to draw.

  3. It may be possible to keep certain assets (e.g. property used by the business) outside the company.

- Other benefits: provide tax-free benefits to your employees such as childcare, sports or recreation facilities.

For those moving house while changing jobs

If you move home in order to take up new employment, or even a new post within your existing organisation, the following costs can be reimbursed by your employer without any Income Tax charge arising, up to an overall maximum of £8,000:

1. Bridging finance

2. Legal and professional fees and Stamp Duty

3. Travel and hotel costs

4. A reasonable subsistence allowance

5. A disturbance allowance (e.g. removal costs and insurance)

For those about to retire or who are retired

Golden handshakes – advance tax planning

- You might ask your employer to pay part of any payment over £30,000 into your pension (within the limits of the scheme). HMRC accepts that no tax charge arises on such payments and this could enhance the tax-free lump sum you receive from the scheme.

- If you are retiring and your total income will be significantly lower after retirement, it may be better to retire shortly after 5 April so that the taxable part of your golden handshake may be charged at a lower tax rate.

For the over 65s

- Do remember that age allowance (a higher personal allowance) is available for those aged 65, and for those over 75 there is a higher age allowance available.

For the self-employed

The self-employed have considerably more flexibility in their tax-saving arrangements than employees, and those who are self-employed are probably well aware of the sort of advantages they may legitimately take. However, here are a few that should not be overlooked:

- If you are starting in business and need to draw all your profit to fund your living expenses, it may not be advisable to form a limited company straight away. As a self-employed trader, you have more flexibility and lower administrative costs. You can always incorporate later.

- A pension scheme is a most efficient way of diverting surplus profits into a tax-free lump sum and pension for the future.

A list of the types of expenses generally allowed is on pages 67 to 72.

For personal taxpayers – particularly higher-rate taxpayers

For those with high income (i.e. into the 40 per cent tax band), and particularly if it's surplus to requirements, funds can be diverted to the following havens for tax advantages either on initial payment or at a later date:

- Life assurance – investing in a 'with profits' endowment policy that will run for at least ten years can produce a good tax-free return.

- National Savings Certificates – these can produce a good tax-free income. It's always a good idea to keep aware of what National Savings Schemes have on offer.

- Perks in quoted shares – many quoted shares now offer perks to their shareholders and these are entirely tax free.

- National Insurance – if you have more than one source of employment earnings and you are in danger of paying more than the maximum, why not defer Class I contributions on one of the employments to avoid making an overpayment?

- Pension contributions.

- The Enterprise Investment Scheme – you can invest up to £500,000 in Enterprise Investment Scheme (EIS) shares and you will get Income Tax relief of 20 per cent on that amount. If you hold the shares for three years, you get full Capital Gains Tax relief on sale (now 18 per cent). There is a minimum investment of £500.

Half of an investment made before 6 October may be carried back to the previous tax year for Income Tax purposes (up to a maximum of £50,000).

You must hold your Enterprise Investment Scheme shares for at least three years or the relief will be withdrawn.

Any loss you make on the sale of the shares is available against either capital gains or income.

You must not be connected with the company (i.e. hold over 30 per cent of the shares or be an employee) although you can become a director of the company and still qualify for EIS relief as long as you were not connected with the company before the shares were issued.

Deferral relief: in addition to the above, if you have made a capital gain this year, and if you reinvest all that gain in the purchase of EIS shares, you can thereby defer all the Capital Gains Tax payable this year on that gain until you sell your EIS shares.

- A Venture Capital Trust (see page 95).

For low earners

Young earners

Young people starting in employment have little scope for tax saving (usually because they have a low income), but they should not overlook the favourable Capital Gains Tax treatment available for those who purchase their main residence. Very few people have ever regretted purchasing their own residence.

Other low earners

Don't forget, if you are a low earner, whether in employment or self-employment, you may be able to avoid either Class 1 or Class 2 National Insurance contributions. You should not claim exemption from Class 2 contributions on the basis of low earnings unless you are already paying contributions on another source of income. If you don't pay, you build up no entitlement to benefits or pension rights. £2.30 per week is a small sum to pay to safeguard this entitlement. See page 29.

Tax-savings tips for children

Surplus after-tax income transferred by parents to their children is usually non-taxable in the hands of the child. However, where children earn income exceeding £100 in any tax year on capital provided by their parents, the whole income will be counted as that of their parents.

Make sure that savings accounts with building societies or banks in children's names are paying interest gross. Ask the bank for, and complete, Form R85, which certifies the children as non-taxpayers.

The Child Trust Fund is a tax-free savings scheme designed for children. The Government contributes £250 for children born on or after 1 September 2002 and a further £250 (£500 for lower-income families) at the age of seven. Parents, family and friends can contribute a further £1,200 annually. The child is entitled to the fund at the age of 18 and there will be no restriction on how they use the money.

Capital Gains Tax planning

Note: Spouses include same-sex couples who have registered as civil partners.

- For married couples each spouse will be taxed on their own gains and will receive a non-transferable annual exemption of £9,600.

- Do remember to maximise the benefit of your annual exemptions. To this end you could delay disposals until after the next 5 April if you have already used your current exemption or, alternatively, bring forward planned disposals to before 6 April if you have not yet used your exemption, or split the disposals of some asset, such as blocks of shares, to straddle 5 April in order to obtain the benefit of two years' exemptions.

- Consider whether you can wait until after 5 April to make the sales so as to delay the tax payment by a further 12 months.

- Assets of negligible value: if you hold an asset (e.g. shares in a company) which has lost most of its value, you may be able to claim the capital loss now against any capital gains. Ask your tax inspector if they will allow the loss.

- Loans and guarantees: you may obtain relief for losses on loans and guarantees made to people who have used the money wholly for the purpose of their business. Relief is not available if the loss or guarantee arises through your own act or omission or where the borrower is your husband or wife.

- No capital gain or loss arises on gifts between husband and wife, but the recipient takes over the other spouse's acquisition date and original value.

- Gifts to charities: because these are exempt from Capital Gains Tax it's often better, if you intend making a charitable donation of an asset which would realise a gain on disposal (e.g. shares), to consider donating the asset rather than the equivalent amount of cash. The charity may subsequently sell the shares and realise the gain free of tax because of its privileged status.

- Holdover relief for gifts: this is restricted to business assets, heritage property and property on which there is an immediate charge to Inheritance Tax.

- Don't always claim holdover relief – it's sometimes cheaper to pay a small amount of tax than to hold over the tax bill of some considerably greater sum to the future.

- All gifts are exempt from Stamp Duty.

- If you have assets which you expect will increase in value over a period of time, consider giving them to your children now.

- Main residence: no Capital Gains Tax is payable on the disposal of your home. Taking in a lodger doesn't affect your main residence relief but letting the property can.

Inheritance Tax planning

- Married couples and civil partners should remember the doubling up of the nil-rate band. From 9 October 2007 each couple has a joint tax-free band, £624,000 for 2008-09, which is to increase to £700,000 in 2010-11.

- It's now possible to give away £312,000 every seven years without a charge to Inheritance Tax arising. However, there may be Capital Gains Tax on a non-cash gift, so take professional advice.

- There is tapering relief on the Inheritance Tax attributable to gifts so that, as the years up to seven slip by, the tax bill can reduce significantly. As no tax is attributable to nil-rated gifts, this relief is irrelevant to them.

- It's important to remember, in planning to reduce the Inheritance Tax bill upon your death, not to give away too much unless you can genuinely afford to do so. If you wish to make a gift of your family home but also wish to continue living in it, you must either pay full market rent for the privilege or consult a specialist Inheritance Tax adviser who may be able to provide a sophisticated planning scheme to circumvent the 'reservation of benefit' rules. With no Capital Gains Tax arising on death it's sometimes better to let properties pass on death rather than before. However, this matter must be carefully weighed up before a decision is made.

- Lifetime gifts: gifts between husband and wife are exempt from Inheritance Tax.

- Remember, you can give away the annual Inheritance-Tax-exempt sum of £3,000, which may be doubled up if exemption was not used in the previous year.

- Gifts of up to £250 per year to an individual are tax free.

- Gifts out of surplus income are tax free; take professional advice on this.

- Wedding gifts up to certain limits are tax free.

- Term assurance written in trust is a sensible means of protecting a gift that has been made should tax become due as a result of death within seven years.

- Always make a Will and build the necessary tax planning points into it. Discuss this with your solicitor, but see an Inheritance Tax specialist first.

- Special reliefs. Generally, business assets attract some measure of relief, as does woodland and agricultural property. Agricultural property without a right to vacant possession may attract a lower rate of relief.

- Doubling up the main residence relief. It doesn't make good sense for you to buy a house or flat for your adult children to live in since any gain you make on its subsequent sale will be chargeable to Capital Gains Tax. Instead, consider providing your child with the necessary funds to make the purchase in their own name and you could do this by making an interest-free loan which you reduce each year by the annual £3,000 exemption.

- Incorporation of a growing business. It may be advantageous to give shares in the company to your children and/or grandchildren soon after incorporation when their value is relatively low.

Notable tax dates

See Appendix 11.

What is the difference between tax 'avoidance' and tax 'evasion'?

The short answer is that tax evasion is unlawful and tax avoidance is permissible. An example of tax evasion is deciding not to give HMRC details of all your sales (to pocket the cash and not tell anybody about the sales). This is fraudulent and will be heavily punished by the authorities when they discover it. Tax avoidance is taking the necessary legal measures to reduce your tax liabilities to the lowest permissible figure. For example, you may decide to invest in tax-free investments, such as ISAs, rather than in an investment which produces income that is taxable. However, remember that HMRC has certain anti-avoidance provisions to prevent tax being saved as a result of certain activities (e.g. inventing artificial transactions in land).

How should I deal with the Tax Office?

When we began in practice, some 30 years ago, HMRC's staff were portrayed as ogres and inspectors were regarded as 'the enemy'. In fact, in our long years of practice, we have always found we have enjoyed good relations with the Inspectors of Taxes and these bad reputations were both unkind and totally misleading.

However, our own observations apart, there is no doubt at all that in the last ten years particularly, HMRC has become extremely friendly, helpful and courteous in its dealings. The arrival on the scene of the Taxpayers' Charter is evidence that HMRC is trying to be 'user friendly'.

Accordingly, our advice is that if you find you are dealing with HMRC, even if you are having difficulty making your tax payments, you will find most of the personnel extremely helpful, efficient and courteous and, in return, you are best advised to be efficient, courteous and prompt in your dealings with them.

In 1972, one of our authors had a letter published in the business section of *The Times* which read as follows:

Sir, Mr Jenkins has trouble dealing with the Inspectors of Taxes via his accountant. May I suggest he discontinue to use his accountant as a mediator between him and his inspector? If he were to prepare his various financial statements, which he obviously does for himself anyhow, and submit them in his honesty to the inspector, he will receive help and guidance from a man who is more often than not very understanding and reasonable and, what is more, he won't have to pay for the service.

Should I use an accountant?

The arrival of self-assessment was, we suspect, originally intended to do away with the accountancy profession. After all, self-assessment implies that the tax laws are so simple that you can 'do it yourself'.

The reality, and we feel that the answers given in this book prove that what we are about to say is correct, is that self-assessment has added to the complications and responsibilities and our view is that anyone having to fill out a Tax Return should seriously consider using the services of an accountant. Not only is life more complicated, but there are now penalties which were not in place before the arrival of self-assessment.

When using an accountant you should always:

- ensure that the first meeting is free, so that you don't have to part with any money until you know whether you like the person or not;

- ask them to quote for fees upfront and ask them if it's an all-inclusive service.

For far too long professional accountants and solicitors have churned out bills to their clients based on the hours worked multiplied by the hourly rate. We believe that this approach is totally unfair to the client because the accountant never knows how big the bill is going to be. Instead, we believe that quotations should be made upfront and they should be stuck to, and that the professional should take more risk than has been the case.

How should I handle tax investigations?

HMRC is very successful at collecting additional tax through its tax investigations and we can all expect an HMRC inquiry into our affairs.

Self-assessment has given tax officers the power to make random tax inquiries. In effect, this means that they have more scope than ever to initiate tax investigations as you may now be investigated even if you have kept proper records.

While no taxpayer will be exempt from a random audit (whether they are an individual or a business), if their accounting and tax records are in good order and if the self-assessed tax liabilities have been calculated accurately and paid on time, they should have little to fear.

When you receive notice that an inquiry has begun, you should respond promptly, courteously and co-operatively. We would normally suggest you seek the services of a qualified accountant.

How do I appeal against a tax demand if I think it's too high?

If you think HMRC has made a mistake in your tax calculation, then you should go along and get the staff to explain how they get to the figures.

If you are not satisfied with their explanation, or you think that there must be an underlying problem which needs special attention, then you should consult a professional accountant and they will do the necessary.

Postscript

A call for the Income Tax year to end on a more sensible date than 5 April

Year after year, successive Chancellors of the Exchequer fail to move this year end by five days to 31 March, the year end used for all other UK taxes. There is even a law which says that the Government should end all tax years on 31 March and yet Chancellors have all, so far, failed to attend to this matter.

The facts of the matter are these:

- 5 April was chosen by accident; the date holds no importance at all and there is no intrinsic reason why we have to end our tax year on it. A change is perfectly possible.

- Inspectors of Taxes find 5 April an inconvenient date.

- Taxpayers find it inconvenient and muddling.

- 70 per cent of employers want it to be changed to 31 March.

- All the accounting and tax bodies want the date to be changed.

- Business people find it difficult for a host of reasons.

- The people who write computer programs for PAYE say that it would be easier for all concerned if the Income Tax year ended on 31 March and it would be very easy for them to change it from the present cumbersome system.

- The people who write our tax laws say that to draft the changes to the law to effect this simple change would be no trouble at all.

- The Treasury would even make money in the year of change, but not enough for us to notice paying the extra for this one year.

- Other countries have changed their tax years, some by more than three months, and have experienced no difficulty in changing.

Until 2001, the only reason why this absurd anomaly has not been rectified is the idleness of the civil servants who, over many years, have failed to serve their Ministers by getting on with this matter.

In 2001, even this reason was knocked out of court by HM Revenue & Customs, admitting that there is no reason for not changing. But, having said this, instead of getting on and changing it, it decided not to do so and to wait until we join the Euro. (What joining the Euro has to do with our tax year end is anyone's guess.)

So if you agree with me that it's absurd and ridiculous, not to say embarrassing, for our country to have a tax year that ends on 5 April (we are the only country in the world that uses it), please write to the Chancellor of the Exchequer. Tell him to get his civil servants to put this change into effect and that failure to do so is not an option.

If you do this in sufficient numbers, next Budget Day we may hear of a measure being announced that will be welcomed by everyone.

Hugh Williams FCA

Glossary

Agricultural property relief	This only relates to Inheritance Tax. Either a 50 per cent or 100 per cent reduction in the value of the agricultural land in the UK, Channel Isles or Isle of Man can be applied when listing the asset values for probate or valuing lifetime gifts.
AIM (Alternative Investment Market)	This is a Stock Exchange market whereby investors can deal in shares in unquoted companies. It was previously called the 'Unlisted Securities Market'.
Alimony	Money payable to a former spouse after divorce.
Annuity	An annual payment to an individual, usually resulting from a capital investment. The regular annual sums cease on death. Due to the payment mainly consisting of a return of capital, only a small part of the annuity usually bears tax at the basic rate.
AVCs (Additional Voluntary Contributions)	These are additional contributions by an employee to their employer's approved pension scheme or to a separate pension provider of the employee's choosing (free-standing AVC).
Bare trusts	A bare trust is one in which the beneficiary has an absolute entitlement to the income and the capital at any time.
Basic rate tax	Income Tax at 20 per cent.
Bed & breakfasting	Until the Spring Budget in 1998 it was common practice to take advantage of the annual tax-free Capital Gains Tax exemption by selling sufficient numbers of shares on one day (to realise a modest

	tax-free gain) only to buy them back the following day at more or less the same price. The 1998 Budget made bed & breakfasting ineffective for tax purposes.
Beneficial loans	This is a loan by an employer to an employee at less than the commercial rate of interest.
Benefits in kind	Otherwise known as 'perks' received by a director or an employee which are nearly always taxed as employment income.
Blind Person's Allowance	An allowance of £1,800 which registered blind people can claim.
Bonds	These are investments provided by insurance companies with apparently favourable tax treatment on both annual payment and final maturity. The annual payments and maturities are called 'chargeable events' by the taxman.
Capital allowances	These allowances are given to businesses for the purchase of capital assets (usually industrial buildings, plant, machinery and motor vehicles) whereby the cost of the assets can be written down against tax over a period of years.
Capital Gains Tax	This is a tax on either the sale or gift of an asset, charging to tax the difference between the original cost and the value (sale proceeds) at disposal. If you make any capital gains as an individual, the first £9,600 gain are exempt from Capital Gains Tax.
Chargeable event	See Bonds.
Class 1A National Insurance contributions	These are special National Insurance contributions payable by employers on employees' benefits.
Corporation Tax	This is a tax levied on profits of limited companies.
Covenants	A payment under a deed of covenant in favour of a charity will normally benefit the charity in that the basic rate tax paid by the individual can usually be reclaimed by the charity, thereby adding to its income – replaced by Gift Aid.

Director	A director is someone appointed by the shareholders to run a limited company. Sometimes people who are not called directors, nor formally appointed as such, by virtue of the activities they undertake in running the business, take on the same responsibilities and liabilities that a formal director attracts. Directors have certain extra responsibilities under tax law, particularly having to report on the taxable benefits they receive.
Discretionary trust	This is a type of trust whereby the trustees are given discretion as to the way in which they distribute income and capital to the various potential beneficiaries. In the case of other (non-discretionary) trusts the trustees are bound to pay the income over to the named beneficiaries.
Dividends	A dividend is a cash sum paid out of profits to shareholders of a company based on the number of shares they hold.
Domicile	Professional advice should be sought over this, but someone who has a foreign domicile doesn't regard the UK as their real home.
Earned income	This is the income of an individual which is derived from their physical, personal or mental labours. It also includes most pensions.
Emoluments	This is a formal name given to salary, remuneration, bonuses and other income deriving from an employment of a director or employee.
Endowment	This usually is a form of life insurance involving payment by the insurer of a sum on a specified date, or on death.
Endowment mortgage	This is a mortgage linked to an endowment insurance policy with the mortgage being repaid from the sum insured.
Enterprise Investment Scheme	This is a scheme under which individuals receive favourable Income Tax and Capital Gains Tax treatment when investing in qualifying unquoted trading companies.

Filing date	31 January, being the date following the end of the tax year by which your Self-Assessment Tax Return must have been submitted to HM Revenue & Customs if you are to avoid an automatic £100 penalty.
Free-Standing AVCs	See AVCs.
Fringe benefits	See Benefits in kind.
General Commissioners	Ordinary people who hear tax appeals and decide either in favour of the taxpayer or the Tax Inspector.
Gift Aid	Whereas deeds of covenant must be written to last at least four years, Gift Aid covers individual single donations to charities from which, so long as basic rate tax has been deducted, the charity is entitled to reclaim the tax. A form has to be obtained from HM Revenue & Customs, filled in and handed to the charity.
Golden handshake	Term given to a lump sum payment made by an employer to an employee on the cessation of their employment. This can usually attract favourable tax treatment.
Gross income	Income from which no tax is deducted at source, even though tax may still have to be paid.
Higher-paid employee	Anyone paid over the surprisingly small sum of £8,500 (including taxable benefits).
Higher-rate tax	Income Tax at 40 per cent.
Holdover relief	This is tax relief given to a donor, or other transferor of business assets, whereby the gain is not charged to tax but deducted from the cost of the asset in the hands of the recipient.
Income Tax	This was the tax introduced in 1799 to pay for the Napoleonic wars and is still with us today.
Indexation allowance	Now available only to companies. This allowance provides for that element of a capital gain which is attributable to inflation.
Inheritance Tax	This is the tax payable on assets transferred on death and by way of lifetime gift, although estates

(including transfers in the previous seven years) don't pay tax on the first £312,000.

Inheritance Tax exemption	It's possible to give away £3,000 each year (the annual exemption) with no Inheritance Tax implications. If you did not use the previous year's exemption it's also possible to go back one year and include that as well, thereby doubling up the exemption to £6,000.
ISA (Individual Savings Account)	A tax-free savings account introduced by the Labour Government and launched on 6 April 1999.
Lodgers	See Rent-a-room relief.
Lower-paid employees	Anyone receiving less than £8,500 per year including benefits in kind.
Lower-rate tax	Income Tax at ten per cent (for savings income only on the first £2,320 of taxable income). If an individual's taxable non-savings income is above this limit, the savings rate is not applicable. There are no changes to the ten per cent dividend rate.
Maintenance	A term for the payments made by one spouse to another after divorce.
MIRAS	The acronym for 'mortgage interest relief deducted at source'.
Mortgage	A debt secured by a document (called a 'mortgage deed') which gives security to the lender for the debt. The mortgage deed must be returned at the time of settlement of the debt.
National Insurance	This is a 'tax' applied to employment income and self-employment income, the contributions going towards the state pension on retirement and other contributory benefits.
Overlap relief	Where a self-employed business suffers tax more than once on a particular year's profits, a figure of overlap relief should be calculated so that, in due course, usually on the cessation of the business, this overpayment of tax may be taken into account.

PAYE (Pay As You Earn)	The compulsory system for employers to use whereby tax is deducted more or less evenly over the year resulting in the correct amount of tax being paid by the end of the tax year on an individual's earnings.
Potentially exempt transfer	A gift made by an individual that, so long as the donor lives for a further seven years, won't attract Inheritance Tax.
Private residence relief	This is the relief that exempts any gain on the sale of the home of an individual from Capital Gains Tax.
Rent-a-room relief	Special relief for individuals who let rooms to lodgers in their homes.
Rollover relief	This is a Capital Gains Tax relief that is available to an individual, partnership or company which disposes of one business asset and uses the proceeds to acquire a replacement business asset during a specified qualifying period.
Self-employed	Someone who is working in business on their own, preparing accounts and paying their own tax and National Insurance contributions. Note: it's often a moot point as to whether somebody is self-employed or employed and professional advice should be sought.
Settlement	See Trust.
Share options	This is an option granted to directors or employees whereby they may buy shares in the company for which they work.
Stamp Duty	This is the duty payable on transfers of shares and properties.
Tax avoidance	Legally arranging your affairs in such a way as to reduce your tax liability.
Tax evasion	Illegally avoiding a tax liability – evade tax at your peril!
Term assurance	This is a cheap form of life assurance whereby, on the death of an individual within a certain specified time, a capital sum will be paid. This can be useful for providing for possible Inheritance Tax liabilities.

Trust (otherwise known as settlement)	Property is held in trust where the owner has passed it to trustees who hold it and manage it under the terms of the legal deed (called the 'trust deed') for the benefit of the beneficiaries.
Unearned income	Income from investments as opposed to income earned.
Unincorporated business	Partnerships and sole traders are unincorporated businesses. Limited liability partnerships and limited companies are incorporated businesses.
Unit trusts	An investment fund investing the combined contributions from individual investors and paying them dividends in proportion to their holdings.
Venture Capital Trusts	This is a type of investment trust for investing in unquoted trading companies with significant tax advantages for the investor.
Wasting assets	This is an asset that has an anticipated useful life of less than 50 years.
Wayleaves	The land and property income deriving from sundry items such as telegraph and electricity poles.
Will	A legal document that shows how a deceased person wished their estate to be distributed, and who was to administer that estate.

Appendices

Appendix 1: Tax rates and allowances at a glance

In 2008/09, the following rates, etc., apply

Income Tax	Band	Taxable Income From	To	Rate
	Basic Rate	0	34,800	20%
	Higher Rate	34,801		40%

Capital Gains Tax (for individuals)		First	9,600	Exempt
	New single rate of 18% plus new entrepreneurs' relief			

Corporation Tax	Band	From	To	Rate
	Small Companies Rate	1	300,000	21%
	Marginal Relief	300,001	1,500,000	29.75%
	Main Rate	1,500,000		28%

Inheritance Tax (on death)	Band	From	To	Rate
	Nil Rate Band	0	312,000	0%
	Over Nil Rate Band	312,000		40%

Personal Allowances		
	Personal	6,035
	Personal (aged 65 to 74)	9,030
	Married Couples (aged less than 75)*#	6,535
	Personal (aged over 75)	9,180
	Married Couples (aged over 75)*#	6,625

All 2 higher age allowances are only available for incomes up to £21,800 in 2008/09
* = relief restricted to 10%   # = husband or wife must be born before 6 April 1935

National Insurance Class 1 (Employment)	Earnings per week	
	Employee (not contracted out)	
	Up to £105	Nil
	£105 to £770	11%
	Over £770	1%
	Employer (not contracted out)	
	Up to £105	Nil
	Over £105	12.8%

Class 2 (Self-Employment)	(The old weekly stamp)			£2.30
	No contributions due if profits below £4,825			

Class 4 (Self-Employment)	8% on profits between	£5,435	and	£40,040
	1% on profits over £40,040			

State Pension		Week	Year
	Single	90.70	£4,716.40
	Married	145.05	£7,542.60
	Age addition (over 80)	0.25	£13.00

VAT		
	Threshold with effect from 1 April	£67,000
	Rate	17.5%

Stamp Duty	From/to	0	150,000	Nil
	From/to	150,001	250,000	1%
	From/to	250,001	500,000	3%
	From/to	500,000		4%

Taxable Car Benefits	*Fuel Benefit*	As with Car Benefit, the taxable charge is based on CO_2 emissions. The charge is based on a sum of £16,900 for all cars, not on the price of the car.
	Car Benefit	The scale charge is based on CO_2 emissions. The Annual Charge ranges from 10% for eco-friendly cars to 35% for Gas Guzzlers. Alternative rates apply to cars registered before 1.1.1998. Diesels attract a 3% surcharge, but not over 35% and not if they are Euro 4 compliant and registered before 6.4.06.
	Van Benefit	

	Van Scale Charge	£3,000
	Fuel Scale Charge for Vans	£500

Car Mileage Allowance		All Engine Sizes
	Up to 10,000 miles pa	40p
	Over 10,000 miles pa	25p

Appendix 1: Tax rates and allowances at a glance (continued)

In 2007/08, the following rates, etc., apply

Income Tax		Band	Taxable Income From	To	Rate
		Starting Rate	0	2,230	10%
		Basic Rate	2,231	34,600	22%
		Higher Rate	34,601		40%

Capital Gains Tax (for individuals)			First	9,200	Exempt
	Balance taxed at 20% and/or 40%				
	Taper relief for long-term gains				

Corporation Tax		Band	From	To	Rate
		Small Companies Rate	1	300,000	20%
		Marginal Relief	300,001	1,500,000	32.5%
		Main Rate	1,500,000		30%

Inheritance Tax (on death)		Band	From	To	Rate
		Nil Rate Band	0	300,000	0%
		Over Nil Rate Band	300,000		40%

Personal Allowances		
	Personal	5,225
	Personal (aged 65 to 74)	7,550
	Married Couples (aged 65 to 74)*#	6,285
	Personal (aged over 75)	7,690
	Married Couples (aged over 75)*#	6,365

All 2 higher age allowances are only available for incomes up to £20,900 in 2007/08
* = relief restricted to 10%   # = husband or wife must be born before 6 April 1935

National Insurance Class 1 (Employment)	Earnings per week			
	Employee (not contracted out)			
	Up to £100			Nil
	£100 to £670			11%
	Over £670			1%
	Employer (not contracted out)			
	Up to £100			Nil
	Over £100			12.8%
Class 2 (Self-Employment)	(The old weekly stamp)			£2.20
	No contributions due if profits below £4,635			
Class 4 (Self-Employment)	8% on profits between	£5,225	and	£34,840
	1% on profits over £34,840			

State Pension		Week	Year
	Single	87.30	£4,539.60
	Married	139.60	£7,259.20
	Age addition (over 80)	0.25	£13.00

VAT		
	Threshold with effect from 1 April	£64,000
	Rate	17.5%

Stamp Duty				
	From/to	0	125,000	Nil
	From/to	125,001	250,000	1%
	From/to	250,001	500,000	3%
	From/to	500,000		4%

Taxable Car Benefits	*Fuel Benefit*	As with Car Benefit, the taxable charge is based on CO_2 emissions. The charge is based on a sum of £14,400 for all cars, not on the price of the car.
	Car Benefit	The scale charge is based on CO_2 emissions. The Annual Charge ranges from 15% for eco-friendly cars to 35% for Gas Guzzlers. There is no adjustment for the age of the car, nor for business mileage driven. Alternative rates apply to cars registered before 1.1.1998. Diesels attract a 3% surcharge, but not over 35% and not if they are Euro 4 compliant and registered before 6.4.06.

	Van Benefit	Any Age of Vehicle
	Van Scale Charge	£3,000
	Fuel Scale Charge for Vans	£500

Car Mileage Allowance		All Engine Sizes
	Up to 10,000 miles pa	40p
	Over 10,000 miles pa	25p

Appendix 2: Checklist of what to keep for your Tax Return

For Income Tax

If you receive...	Keep your...
☐ **Salary/wages**	Payslips (supplied by your employer) P60 (annual statement of earnings from your employer) Notice of coding (issued by HM Revenue & Customs)
☐ **Benefits in kind** (e.g. company car, medical insurance)	P11D (annual statement of benefits) and expense payments from your employer
☐ **State benefits** (e.g. Jobseeker's Allowance, Carer's Allowance, etc.)	Statements of payments to you by the Department for Work and Pensions (DWP)
☐ **Pensions** State pension, other pensions	Statement of pension payments by the Department for Work and Pensions (DWP) or pension funds, etc.
☐ **Share options** (offered by some employers)	Share option documents from your employer
☐ **Other earnings** Tips, commissions and other earnings	Relevant vouchers
☐ **Expenses not reimbursed** by your employer	Expense receipts
☐ **Self-employment and partnerships** Income from self-employment	Self-employed or partnership accounts
☐ **Savings and deposit accounts** Banks Building Societies National Savings	 Bank interest certificates Building Society interest certificates National Savings interest details

Appendix 2: Checklist of what to keep for your Tax Return (continued)

☐ **Share holdings**
Dividends   Dividend vouchers
Unit Trusts   Unit Trust vouchers

☐ **Other sources**
Annuities   Annuity vouchers
Other   Relevant vouchers

☐ **Land and property**
Holiday accommodation   Copy invoices or receipts for rental
Furnished lettings (including   income, etc.
Rent-a-room)   Receipts or supporting evidence of
Wayleaves (e.g. electricity poles) expenditure

If you receive income from...   **Keep your...**

☐ **Overseas**   Foreign income documents (i.e.
                                    dividends, pensions and interest)
                                    Foreign property income

☐ **Trusts and settlements**   Trust tax vouchers (R185), issued by
                                    trustees

☐ **Other sources** such as:
Alimony   Alimony details
Royalties   Royalty income and expenses
Bonds, etc.   Bonds (called 'chargeable events'), etc.

Deductions to claim against Income Tax

☐ **Interest**   Loan interest statements

☐ **Venture Capital Trust shares** Venture Capital Trust certificates

☐ **Enterprise Investment**   Enterprise Investment Scheme
Scheme subscriptions   certificates

☐ **Charitable covenants**   Deeds of covenant

☐ **Gift Aid**   Gift Aid details

Appendix 2: Checklist of what to keep for your Tax Return (continued)

☐ **Death benefits to trade union or friendly society**   Death benefit papers

☐ Or if you are **registered blind**   Relevant papers

For Capital Gains Tax

☐ **Shares**   Contract notes from your stockbroker

☐ **Land and property**   Estate agents' particulars
Completion statements (from solicitors)

☐ **Paintings or other works of art**   Auction advice slips
Sales catalogues

☐ **Businesses** or parts of them   Completion statements from professional advisers

Appendix 3: HM Revenue & Customs Form P11D Expenses and Benefits 2007/08

HM Revenue & Customs

P11D EXPENSES AND BENEFITS 2007–08

Please ensure your entries are clear on both sides of the form.

Employer name

Employer PAYE reference

Employee name

Surname

Forename(s)

Works number/department

National Insurance number

Note to employer
Complete this return for a director, or an employee who earned at a rate of £8,500 a year or more during the year to 5 April 2008. Send the completed form to your HM Revenue & Customs office by 6 July 2008.

Note to employee
Your employer has filled in this form, keep it in a safe place. You will need it to complete your 2007–08 Tax Return if you get one. The box numberings on this P11D are the same as on the Employment Page of the Tax Return for example, 13.

If a director tick here ▶

Date of birth *in figures (if known)*
D D M M Y Y Y Y

Gender M – Male F – Female

Employers pay Class 1A National Insurance contributions on most benefits. These are shown in boxes which are brown and have a **1A** indicator

A Assets transferred (cars, property, goods or other assets)

Description of asset

| Cost/Market value | Amount made good or from which tax deducted | Cash equivalent |
| £ | £ | 13 £ |

B Payments made on behalf of employee

Description of payment

15 £

Tax on notional payments not borne by employee within 90 days of receipt of each notional payment

15 £

C Vouchers or credit cards

Value of vouchers and payments made using credit cards or tokens (for qualifying childcare vouchers the excess over £55 a week)

| Gross amount | Amount made good or from which tax deducted | Cash equivalent |
| £ | £ | 12 £ |

D Living accommodation

Cash equivalent of accommodation provided for employee, or his/her family or household

Cash equivalent
14 £

E Mileage allowance and passenger payments

Amount of car and mileage allowances paid to employee for business travel in employee's own vehicle, and passenger payments, in excess of maximum exempt amounts (*See P11D Guide for 2007–08 exempt rates*)

Taxable amount
12 £

F Cars and car fuel *If more than two cars were made available, either at the same time or in succession, please give details on a separate sheet*

	Car 1	Car 2
Make and Model		
Date first registered	/ /	/ /
Approved CO$_2$ emissions figure for cars registered on or after 1 January 1998 Tick box if the car does not have an approved CO$_2$ figure	g/km *See P11D Guide for details of cars that have no approved CO$_2$ figure*	g/km *See P11D Guide for details of cars that have no approved CO$_2$ figure*
Engine size	cc	cc
Type of fuel or power used *Please use the key letter shown in the P11D Guide*		
Dates car was available *Do not complete the 'From' box if the car was available on 5 April 2007 or the 'To' box if it continued to be available on 6 April 2008*	From / / to / /	From / / to / /
List price of car *including car and standard accessories only; if there is no list price, or if it is a classic car, employers see booklet 480*	£	£
Accessories *All non-standard accessories, see P11D Guide*	£	£
Capital contributions (maximum £5,000) the employee made towards the cost of car or accessories	£	£
Amount paid by employee for private use of the car	£	£
Date free fuel was withdrawn *Tick if reinstated in year (see P11D Guide)*	/ /	/ /
Cash equivalent of each car	£	£ 9 £

Total cash equivalent of all cars available in 2007–08

Cash equivalent of fuel for each car | £ | £

Total cash equivalent of fuel for all cars available in 2007–08

10 £

P11D(2008) HMRC 09/07

Appendix 3: HM Revenue & Customs Form P11D Expenses and Benefits 2007/08 (continued)

G Vans

Total cash equivalent of all vans available in 2007–08 — **9** £ [1A]

Total cash equivalent of fuel for all vans available in 2007–08 — **10** £ [1A]

H Interest-free and low interest loans
If the total amount outstanding on all loans does not exceed £5,000 at any time in the year, there is no need to complete this section.

	Loan 1	Loan 2
Number of joint borrowers *(if applicable)*		
Amount outstanding at 5 April 2007 or at date loan was made if later	£	£
Amount outstanding at 5 April 2008 or at date loan was discharged if earlier	£	£
Maximum amount outstanding at any time in the year	£	£
Total amount of interest paid by the borrower in 2007–08 – enter "NIL" if none was paid	£	£
Date loan was made in 2007–08 if applicable	/ /	/ /
Date loan was discharged in 2007–08 if applicable	/ /	/ /
Cash equivalent of loans after deducting any interest paid by the borrower	**15** £ [1A]	**15** £ [1A]

I Private medical treatment or insurance

	Cost to you	Amount made good or from which tax deducted	Cash equivalent
Private medical treatment or insurance	£ –	£ =	**11** £ [1A]

J Qualifying relocation expenses payments and benefits
Non-qualifying benefits and expenses go in sections M and N below

Excess over £8,000 of all qualifying relocation expenses payments and benefits for each move — **15** £ [1A]

K Services supplied

	Cost to you	Amount made good or from which tax deducted	Cash equivalent
Services supplied to the employee	£ –	£ =	**15** £ [1A]

L Assets placed at the employee's disposal

	Annual value plus expenses incurred	Amount made good or from which tax deducted	Cash equivalent
Description of asset	£ –	£ =	**13** £ [1A]

M Other items (including subscriptions and professional fees)

	Cost to you	Amount made good or from which tax deducted	Cash equivalent
Description of other items	£ –	£ =	**15** £ [1A]
Description of other items	£ –	£ =	**15** £

	Tax paid
Income tax paid but not deducted from director's remuneration	**15** £

N Expenses payments made to, or on behalf of, the employee

	Cost to you	Amount made good or from which tax deducted	Taxable payment
Travelling and subsistence payments *(except mileage allowance payments for employee's own car - see section E)*	£ –	£ =	**16** £
Entertainment *(trading organisations read P11D Guide and then enter a tick or a cross as appropriate here)*	£ –	£ =	**16** £
General expenses allowance for business travel	£ –	£ =	**16** £
Payments for use of home telephone	£ –	£ =	**16** £
Non-qualifying relocation expenses *(those not shown in sections J or M)*	£ –	£ =	**16** £
Description of other expenses	£ –	£ =	**16** £

Appendix 4: A template to help you prepare your figures for the self-employed part of the Tax Return

Your name _____ Accounting year end _____

Self-employment and Partnerships

Sales income A

less Costs of sales, e.g. raw materials and stocks

Construction industry subcontractors' costs

Other direct costs, e.g. packing and despatch

Total cost of sales B

Gross profit or loss A – B C

Other income D

Expenditure

Employee costs
Salaries, wages, bonuses, employer's NIC, pension contributions, casual wages, canteen costs, recruitment agency fees, subcontractors (unless shown above) and other wages costs

Premises costs
Rent, ground rent, rates, water, refuse, light and heat, property insurance, security and use of home

Repairs
Repair of property, replacements, renewals, maintenance

General administrative expenses
Telephone, fax, mobile telephone, stationery, photocopying, printing, postage, courier and computer costs, subscriptions, insurance

Motoring expenses
Petrol, servicing, licence, repairs, motor insurance, hire and leasing, car parking, RAC/AA membership

Travel and subsistence
Rail, air, bus, etc., travel, taxis, subsistence and hotel costs

Entertainment
Staff entertaining (e.g. Christmas party), customer gifts up to £50 per person advertising your business

Advertising and promotion
Advertising, promotion, mailshots, free samples, brochures, newsletters, trade shows, etc.

Legal and professional costs
Accountancy, legal, architects, surveyors, stocktakers' fees, indemnity insurance

Bad debts (if already included in A above)

Interest
on bank loans, overdraft and other loans

Other finance charges
Bank charges, HP interest, credit card charges, leasing not already included

Depreciation and losses on sale (please ask for advice)

Other items – please describe

Grand total of expenses E

Net profit (or loss) C + D – E

Appendix 5: Gift Aid declaration

Name of Charity:

Details of Donor:

Title _____ Forename(s) _____

Surname _____

Address _____

_____

_____

_____ Postcode _____

I want the charity to treat

       * the enclosed donation of £ _____

       * the donation(s) of £ _____ which I made on _____ / _____ / _____

       * all donations I make from the date of this declaration until I notify you otherwise

       * all donations I have made since 6 April 2000, and all donations I make from the date of this declaration until I notify you otherwise

as Gift Aid donations.

delete as appropriate

Notes
1. You can cancel this declaration at any time by notifying the charity.
2. You must pay an amount of Income Tax and/or Capital Gains Tax at least equal to the tax that the charity reclaims on your donations in the tax year (currently 28p for each £1 you give).
3. If, in the future, your circumstances change and you no longer pay tax on your income and capital gains equal to the tax that the charity reclaims, you can cancel your declaration (see note 1).
4. If you pay at the higher rate, you can claim further tax relief in your Self-Assessment Tax Return.
5. If you are unsure of whether your donations qualify for Gift Aid tax relief, ask the charity or ask your local Tax Office for leaflet IR113 *Gift Aid*.

Appendix 6: A template to help you prepare your figures for the land and property income part of the Tax Return

Your name _____

Land and Property Income (year to 5 April   )

Income	Received from	Rents received £

_____

_____

_____

Total income £ _____

Tax already deducted from property income £

		£	£

Expenditure

Premises Rents _____
Rates _____
Property insurance _____
Light and heat _____
Cleaning _____
Security _____
Subtotal [   ]

Repairs and maintenance Repairs and renewals _____
Redecorating _____
Small tools _____
Subtotal [   ]

Finance charges and interest on loan to buy rented property [   ]

Legal and professional Legal _____
Accountancy _____
Debt collection _____
Other insurances _____
Subscriptions _____
Architects' fees _____
Subtotal [   ]

Services provided Wages _____
Telephone _____
TV _____
Garden _____
Roads _____
Subtotal [   ]

Other costs Advertising _____
Agents' fees _____
Office costs _____
Travel _____
Subtotal [   ]

Total expenditure £ [   ]

Appendix 7: A rough guide to Capital Gains Tax and Inheritance Tax
(see Notes on the following page)

The effect of a .... of following items on	Gift — CGT	Gift — IHT	Sale — CGT	Sale — IHT	Death — CGT	Death — IHT
Own residence	None	Normally none, but donee must retain assets for seven years and donor must survive seven years.	None	None	None	Taxable – see note 3
Business assets:						
Land used in business	Taxable		Taxable	None	None	There should be 100% relief.
Goodwill	Taxable		Taxable	None	None	
Furnished lettings	Taxable		Taxable	None	None	
Partnerships	Taxable		Taxable	None	None	
Other assets	Taxable		Taxable	None	None	
Milk, etc. quotas	Taxable		Taxable	None	None	
Woodlands	Not taxable†		Not taxable†	None	None	See note 4
Shares in small business	Taxable		Taxable	None	None	
Let property subject to:						
Gladstone vs. Bowers tenancies	Taxable – see note 1		Taxable – see note 1	None	None	Should be 100% relief
Residential tenancies	Taxable – see note 2		Taxable – see note 2	None	None	Taxable – see note 3
Farm business tenancies	Taxable – see note 1		Taxable – see note 1	None	None	Should be 100% relief
Other business tenancies	Taxable – see note 1		Taxable – see note 1	None	None	Should be 50% relief
Heritage properties	Normally taxable – see note 5	Tapering relief* after three years	Normally taxable	None	None	Not taxable
Works of art	Taxable – see note 2		Taxable – see note 2	None	None	Taxable – see note 3
Loans to a business	Should be no CGT		Should be no CGT	None	None	Taxable – see note 3
Stock Exchange investments	Taxable – see note 2		Taxable – see note 2	None	None	Taxable – see note 3
Lloyds investments	Taxable – see note 1		Taxable – see note 1	None	None	Should be 100% relief
Trusts (interest in possession)	Not applicable	N/A	Not applicable	N/A	None	Taxable – see note 3

> **This is only a rough guide; professional advice MUST be sought before taking action**

*Tapering relief tax charge: Death within 3 years – 100%; death within 3–4 years – 80%; death within 4–5 years – 60%; death within 5–6 years – 40%; death within 6–7 years – 20%; death after 7 years – 0%

†Standing or felled trees do not attract CGT but the land itself is subject to it

Appendix 7: A rough guide to Capital Gains Tax and Inheritance Tax
(continued)

Notes to Appendix 7

Note 1

Disposals of business assets are subject to a number of Capital Gains Tax reliefs but seek professional advice, because this is only a brief summary:

EIS deferral relief – an investment in shares in an unquoted trading company defers the gain. The acquisition cost is reduced by the gain.

Rollover relief – where the disposal of business assets leads to replacement business assets being acquired, the gain on disposal is not charged to tax but the cost of the new assets is reduced by the gain.

Capital Gains Tax annual exemption – £9,600.

Note 2

The following are ways in which Capital Gains Tax may be reduced or legally avoided:

EIS deferral relief – an investment in shares in an unquoted trading company defers the gain. The acquisition cost is reduced by the gain.

Capital Gains Tax annual exemption – £9,600.

Business losses – trading losses may be set against capital gains of that year or of the previous year, but only if they have first been set against the individual's general income for that year. Capital gains can only be offset against the previous year if the business has been carried out in the previous year.

Enterprise Investment Schemes (EIS) – an annual investment of up to £500,000 secures Income Tax relief of 20 per cent. Capital Gains Tax deferral relief of 18 per cent will be available on EIS.

Venture Capital Trust (VCT) – an annual investment of up to £200,000 secures Income Tax relief of 30 per cent.

Note 3

Assets passing on death normally attract Inheritance Tax at 40 per cent, but the first £312,000 is tax free. Also, transfers to the spouse of the deceased are normally exempt.

Note 4

Property used in a business which is owned by a partner or property used in a business which is controlled by the shareholder attracts only 50 per cent relief. The property must have been used and owned for two years. Shares giving control in an agricultural company attract 100 per cent relief. Shares in a private company attract 100 per cent relief. Controlling shareholdings in quoted companies attract 50 per cent relief.

Note 5

There may be holdover relief available.

This is only a rough guide; professional advice MUST be sought before taking action

Appendix 8: Foreign income and residence issues explained

Residence and tax issues explained
What income, etc., do you pay tax on?

If you are:	Rent arising		Salary arising		Pension arising		Interest arising		Dividends arising		Self-employment income		Capital Gains*		Inheritance Tax on assets	
	In UK	Outside UK	In UK	Outside UK	In UK	Outside UK	In UK	Outside UK	In UK	Outside UK	In UK	Outside UK	In UK	Outside UK	In UK	Outside UK
Resident and ordinarily resident	UK Taxable	UK Taxable	UK Taxable	UK Taxable	UK Taxable	UK Taxable up to 90%	UK Taxable	UK Taxable	UK Taxable	UK Taxable	UK Taxable	UK Taxable	UK Taxable	UK Taxable	Taxable	Depends on Domicile
Resident but not ordinarily resident	UK Taxable	UK Taxable if Received in UK	UK Taxable	UK Taxable if Received in UK	UK Taxable	UK Taxable as to 90% if Received in UK	UK Taxable	UK Taxable if Received in UK	UK Taxable if Received in UK	UK Taxable if Received in UK	UK Taxable	UK Taxable if Received in UK	UK Taxable	UK Taxable	Taxable	Depends on Domicile
Not resident	UK Taxable	Not Taxable	UK Taxable	Not Taxable	UK Taxable	Not Taxable	UK Taxable	Not Taxable	UK Taxable	Not Taxable	UK Taxable	Not Taxable	UK Tax Free	UK Tax Free	Taxable	Depends on Domicile
UK domiciled	Depends on Residence	Depends on Residence	Depends on Residence	Depends on Residence	Depends on Residence	Depends on Residence	Depends on Residence	Depends on Residence	Depends on Residence	Depends on Residence	Depends on Residence	Depends on Residence	Depends on Residence	Depends on Residence	UK Taxable	UK Taxable
Not UK domiciled	Depends on Residence	Depends on Residence	Depends on Residence	Depends on Residence	Depends on Residence	Depends on Residence	Depends on Residence	Depends on Residence	Depends on Residence	Depends on Residence	Depends on Residence	Depends on Residence	Depends on Residence	Depends on Residence	UK Taxable	UK Tax Free

In principle – but please take advice because this area is a minefield – the following notes should be helpful:

Most people living in UK will be 'resident' and 'ordinarily resident' and 'UK domiciled'.

People born in the UK will be UK domiciled unless they change it.

You normally have to leave the UK for one complete tax year to be non-resident for Income Tax and for five complete tax years to be non-resident for Capital Gains Tax.

Visitors to the UK, who spend more than six months here, will probably be treated as resident but not ordinarily resident.

* Take advice on Capital Gains Tax issues before becoming non-UK resident to save Capital Gains Tax.

From 6 April 2008 non-domiciled, or not ordinarily resident, individuals, who have been in the UK for seven of the last ten years, will continue to be able to access the remittance basis of taxation on payment of an annual £30,000 charge on the foreign income and gains left outside the UK, unless their unremitted foreign gains and income is below £2,000.

Appendix 9: A template to help you work out your Inheritance Tax bill and plan to make a Will

I own	Estimated value	At my death I would like to leave this to:
House		
Valuables		
Shares*		
Cash		
Other land and property		
Trust		
Business assets*		
The residue of my estate		
Legacies I would like to give		Details:
Substantial gifts I have made in the last seven years		Gifted to:
Less Sums I owe	( )	How will these be repaid on death?
Total estate		
Less tax-free band	**(312,000)**	
Less unused tax-free band of deceased spouse/civil partner (only available when the second death is after 8 October 2007)	**(x)**	
Total net		
Tax due @ 40%		

* Some shares (those listed on the Alternative Investment Market and shares in unlisted companies) and business assets will attract 100 per cent business property relief and be effectively free of Inheritance Tax.

Appendix 10: Personal fact sheet

If you were to die today, how would your family and executors find your papers, etc. and sort everything out? This personal fact sheet is a way of helping you and your survivors.

You might like to fill this in, to keep a copy yourself and place a copy with your Will.

A   **Full name** (including title and decorations)

Date of birth   Place of birth

Tax reference no.

State pension no.

National Insurance no.

Others

This personal fact sheet prepared (date)

B   **My Will**

Made on

Reviewed on

Is kept at

My executors are   Tel no.

Tel no.

Tel no.

Tel no.

Appendix 10: Personal fact sheet (continued)

C **Substantial gifts made before death**

Date of gift   Date   Value

_____

_____

D **Location of other key documents**

Funeral wishes _____

Keys to safe _____

Birth certificate _____

Marriage certificate _____

Insurance policies _____

Pension policies _____

Property and mortgage deeds _____

Bank statements _____

Building society passbooks _____

Medical card _____

Car documents _____

Share certificates _____

Other investment certificates _____

Where to find brief biographical details for any obituary
(suggest who else might be able to write this)

_____

_____

Trust deeds _____

Leases of rented property _____

Partnership deed (copy) _____

_____

Appendix 10: Personal fact sheet (continued)

E **People to contact**

Accountant (see back page)

Solicitor

Stockbroker

Insurance broker

Bankers

Pension payer

Tax Office

Employer

Doctor

Trustees

Life assurance

Any other key adviser

F **My business affairs**

Details

Directorships

Partnerships

G **My insurance policies**

On my death the following policies mature   Location

Appendix 10: Personal fact sheet (continued)

H Employment history

From   To   Employer   Address

_____

_____

_____

I My pension arrangements

Pensions payable by _____

_____ Tel no. _____

Annuities I receive _____

_____

J Other assets

Details of other assets not already listed _____

_____

_____

K Liabilities

Debts I owe   Loans _____

Overdrafts _____

HP debts _____

Mortgages _____

Guarantees I have made to _____

on behalf of _____ for £ _____

L Clubs and organisations I belong to

_____

_____

M Who else has a copy of this form?

_____

Appendix 11: Notable tax dates

Date	Significance of Date	Employers	Individual Tax Payers	Partners and Sole Traders
19/4/2008	Deadline for settling 2007/08 PAYE and National Insurance contributions – interest will be charged from this date on overdue balances	✓		
19/5/2008	Deadline date for Payroll Year-End Return – penalty of £100 per month for each 50 employees for any late P35	✓		
31/5/2008	Deadline date for getting P60 forms to employees	✓		
6/7/2008	Deadline date for sending P11D forms to employees	✓		
	Deadline date for sending P11D forms and P11D(F) Return of Class 1A National Insurance contributions due to HMRC	✓		
19/7/2008	Payment of Class 1A National Insurance contributions to HMRC	✓	✓	✓
31/7/2008	Second instalments of Income Tax and Class 4 National Insurance re 2007/08 are due		✓	✓
	Another £100 fine for late submission of 2006/07 Tax Return. A further five per cent surcharge where tax due for 2006/07 still outstanding		✓	✓
30/9/2008	Deadline for submission of 2007/08 Tax Return for tax calculation by HMRC		✓	✓
31/10/2008	Deadline for submission of 2007/08 paper Tax Return – for penalty, see next section		✓	✓
31/1/2009	Deadline for electronic submission of 2007/08 Tax Return. Late filers will be charged a £100 fine (and in the case of a late partnership return each partner will be fined £100) and interest on overdue tax		✓	✓
	Balance of tax due for 2007/08		✓	✓
	First payment on account for 2008/09 tax year		✓	✓
28/2/2009	A five per cent surcharge where tax due for 2007/08 still outstanding		✓	✓
5/4/2009	End of 2008/09 tax year	✓	✓	✓

Appendix 11: Notable tax dates (continued)

Date	Significance of Date	Employers	Individual Tax Payers	Partners and Sole Traders
19/4/2009	Deadline for settling 2008/09 PAYE and National Insurance contributions – interest will be charged from this date on overdue balances	✓		
19/5/2009	Deadline date for Payroll Year-End Return – penalty of £100 per month for each 50 employees for any late P35	✓		
31/5/2009	Deadline date for getting P60 forms to employees	✓		
6/7/2009	Deadline date for sending P11D forms to employees	✓		
	Deadline date for sending P11D forms and P11D(F) Return of Class 1A National Insurance contributions due to HMRC	✓		
19/7/2009	Payment of Class 1A National Insurance contributions to HMRC	✓	✓	✓
31/7/2009	Second instalments of Income Tax and Class 4 National Insurance re 2008/09 are due		✓	✓
	Another £100 fine for late submission of 2007/08 Tax Return. A further five per cent surcharge where tax due for 2007/08 still outstanding		✓	✓
30/9/2009	Deadline for submission of 2008/09 Tax Return for tax calculation by HMRC		✓	✓
31/10/2009	Deadline for submission of 2008/09 paper Tax Return – for penalty, see next section		✓	✓
31/1/2010	Deadline for electronic submission of 2008/09 Tax Return. Late filers will be charged a £100 fine (and in the case of a late partnership return each partner will be fined £100) and interest on overdue tax		✓	✓
	Balance of tax due for 2008/09		✓	✓
	First payment on account for 2009/10 tax year		✓	✓
28/2/2010	A five per cent surcharge where tax due for 2008/09 still outstanding		✓	✓

Appendix 12: Tax reliefs available for investment in unquoted companies

Tax reliefs available for investment in unquoted companies

	Income Tax Relief on Amount Invested	Capital Gains Tax Deferral	Tax-Free Income	Tax-Free Gains	Income Tax Relief on Losses	Losses Offsettable against Capital Gains
Purchasing shares directly	No	No	No	No	Yes	Yes
Enterprise Investment Scheme	Yes	Yes	No	Yes	Yes	Yes
Venture Capital Trusts	Yes	No	Yes	Yes	No	No

Appendix 13: Cars with low carbon dioxide emissions

In ascending order, **petrol-engined cars** emitting less than 110g/km CO_2 are:

- Toyota Prius E-CVT (104g/km)
- Honda Civic Hybrid CVT (109g/km)
- Citroën C1 998cc five-speed manual (108g/km)
- Toyota Aygo 998cc five-speed manual or autoclutch (109g/km)
- Peugeot 107 998cc five-speed manual or autoclutch (109g/km)

Diesel options are:

- Seat Ibiza 1.4 Tdi Ecomotion (99g/km)
- VW Polo 1.4 BlueMotion five-speed manual – no A/C (99g/km); with A/C (104g/km)
- Skoda Fabia Estate 1.4 Green Line (109g/km)
- Citroën C1 1,398cc five-speed manual (109g/km)
- Toyota Aygo 1,398cc five-speed manual (109g/km)
- Mini Cooper D Hatch six-speed (104g/km)
- Mini Cooper D Clubman six-speed (109g/km)
- Fiat 500 1.3 Multijet (110g/km)

Appendix 14: VAT Fuel Scale Charges for three-month periods

CO_2 band	VAT Fuel Scale Charge, three-month period £	VAT on three-month charge £	VAT exclusive three-month charge £
140 or below	182.00	27.11	154.89
145	195.00	29.04	165.96
150	207.00	30.83	176.17
155	219.00	32.62	186.38
160	231.00	34.40	196.60
165	243.00	36.19	206.81
170	256.00	38.13	217.87
175	268.00	39.91	228.09
180	280.00	41.70	238.30
185	292.00	43.49	248.51
190	304.00	45.28	258.72
195	317.00	47.21	269.79
200	329.00	49.00	280.00
205	341.00	50.79	290.21
210	353.00	52.57	300.43
215	365.00	54.36	310.64
220	378.00	56.30	321.70
225	390.00	58.09	331.91
230	402.00	59.87	342.13
235	414.00	61.66	352.34
240 or above	426.00	63.45	362.55

Index

This index covers chapters, but not appendices or Glossary. Terms refer to taxation.